Alm

1976

Mother & Doc.

A First Book of Antiques

Cyril Bracegirdle

~~~~~~~~~~~~~~~~

A First
Book of Antiques

~~~~~~~~~~~~~~~~

Illustrated with photographs
and with drawings by Leslie Atkinson

HEINEMANN : LONDON

William Heinemann Ltd
LONDON MELBOURNE TORONTO
JOHANNESBURG AUCKLAND

First published 1970
© Cyril Bracegirdle 1970
Drawings © William Heinemann Ltd 1970
434 92940 9

Printed in Great Britain by
Cox & Wyman Ltd
London, Fakenham and Reading

Illustrations

PHOTOGRAPHS	*facing page*
Robert Adam room at Osterley Park House, Middlesex	68
16th century German dagger	69
Victorian steam toy	69
Worcester porcelain	84
Flint-lock pistols	84
Staffordshire pottery	85
Victorian jewellery	85

DRAWINGS	*page*
Knights in the lists	2
Flintlock gun and swords	13
Classic types of chair	27
Horse brasses and keys	39
Sanctuary door knocker	43
Pottery and porcelain	55
Earthenware and porcelain	63
Choice examples of antique silver	77
Dial hands of long-case clocks	89
A selection of timepieces	91
Coins	99
Victorian jewellery	109
Carved ivory brooch	112
Glass paperweights	116
Victorian dolls	121
Magic Lantern	122

Contents

Foreword: What is an Antique?

1	ARMOUR	1
2	DAGGERS	7
3	FLINT-LOCK PISTOLS AND OTHER FIREARMS	10
4	SWORDS	16
5	CHIPPENDALE AND HIS FURNITURE	21
6	THE AGE OF WALNUT	26
7	SOME MORE FURNITURE	32
8	HORSE BRASSES	37
9	DOOR KNOCKERS AND PORTERS	41
10	LOCKS AND KEYS	45
11	CHINESE PORCELAIN	47
12	MEISSEN PORCELAIN	52
13	SPODE PORCELAIN	57
14	WORCESTER PORCELAIN	59
15	STAFFORDSHIRE POTTERY FIGURES	62

Contents

16	WEDGWOOD POTTERY	68
17	BRITISH SILVER	74
18	OLD SHEFFIELD PLATE	81
19	CLOCKS	87
20	COINS	93
21	VICTORIAN JEWELLERY	104
22	GLASS PAPERWEIGHTS	113
23	TOYS	118
24	HOW AND WHERE TO BUY ANTIQUES	124

Glossary of Terms

General Further Reading

The Antique Periods

Index

Foreword
What is an Antique?

AN antique is an object which is at least 100 years old. It does not have to be beautiful. It may be a homely eighteenth-century kitchen cupboard with little ornamentation, a Victorian copper coal scuttle, or a seventeenth-century blunderbuss, yet all these are valuable because of their age.

Many years ago the United States customs imposed a rule that any item over 100 years old could be imported into America without any import duty having to be paid on it. Influenced by this, the British antique dealers began to classify as antique any object which exceeded the century age limit.

This book describes some of the better-known types of antiques and tells how to recognize them. It also explains how to become a collector.

The subject of antiques is a vast one. It includes pottery, porcelain, silver, glass, furniture, weapons, armour, coins, paintings, carpets, tapestries, clocks, ivories, jewellery, brass, copper and many other things. Within each of these there is a wide range of items. Glass, for instance, includes French paperweights, tumblers, vases, wine glasses, chandeliers, scent bottles, goblets, lamps, bowls and decanters. And there are many kinds of glass: frosted, milk, ruby, lava, *latticino*, moulded, marble, satin, pressed, crackle and many others.

Reading this book will not make you into an expert but it will give you a start and introduce you to a subject which has endless variety.

There has been a tremendous surge of interest in antiques

Foreword

since World War II. This is partly because many people have become better off and now want to decorate their homes with artistic objects which were made by great craftsmen and designers of the past.

As our modern homes become filled with mass-produced items of plastic and chromium so we place a greater value on the handmade treasures of previous centuries, created before the machine age.

Another attraction of antiques is that they are a good investment, for prices are constantly rising. It is comforting to know that the porcelain figure of the shepherdess on the sideboard or that collection of silver snuff-boxes can usually be sold for more than you gave.

To collect antiques successfully you should learn as much as you can about their history and characteristics. Take as your motto *Semper Lego* (read, gather, choose, survey, observe – all these meanings apply).

Always remember that an article which has been restored or re-finished, say a silver tankard with a new handle or a chair with legs that have been broken and repaired or even replaced, is less valuable than if it has survived the years without such work being necessary.

Antiques can be seen in any of hundreds of museums. The Victoria and Albert Museum in London is one of the world's finest treasure houses containing antiques of every description. The Wallace Collection, also in London, has a fine display of French furniture and clocks, and the Fitzwilliam Museum in Cambridge contains one of Britain's biggest collections of ceramics (pottery and porcelain). One may visit the Hanley Museum in Stoke-on-Trent to see Staffordshire pottery, and the museum attached to the Wedgwood factory in Staffordshire for early Wedgwood. Many museums publish booklets describing their treasures and these are a cheap source of information.

Country houses, too, are often of great interest. Harewood House, Yorkshire, has genuine Chippendale furniture,

Foreword

and Woburn Abbey maintains a permanent exhibition of antiques for sale.

In some towns there are evening classes on the study of antiques. Perhaps there is one in your area?

Besides many books there are several magazines available such as *Antique Dealer and Collector's Guide*, *Antique Collector* and the *Art and Antiques Weekly*.

I

Armour

ARMOUR has been worn by fighting men almost ever since tribal conflicts began to be replaced by organized warfare.

Achilles, Hector and the other heroes of Homer's *Iliad* wore shining armour with bright burnished helmets when they fought on the plain before the 'topless towers of Ilium'.

In a later age the Greek soldiers of Alexander's army marched across the lands of Asia Minor and the Fertile Crescent to the very borders of India wearing a body protection called the *cuirass* which had medium-sized plates of bronze. Underneath they wore horsehair coats and flexible leggings. Their heads were protected by large helmets covering their cheeks, and their noses shielded by metal guards.

In the Middle Ages the coat of mail made of interlocking rings was worn. In Europe each ring had four others linked through it and provided a very flexible garment.

Like most protective devices it brought about the invention of new offensive weapons; just as in modern times the armour of a tank provokes the development of armour-piercing shells, so the armour worn by men resulted in the invention of the cross-bow which could pierce the mail with its deadly shafts and long thin knives that could be slipped through the rings.

The answer to these arrived in the fifteenth century in the

form of the breast plate and full body armour. This had to be made carefully to fit each person, and the armourer needed to have the skill of a tailor along with a good knowledge of anatomy. The plates were made from billets of metal hammered flat by hand or sometimes by a water-powered tilt-hammer, but the complete outfits were so expensive that only rich knights could afford them. To keep the armour clean, polished, free from rust and ensure that the complicated arrangement of leather straps and thongs showed no signs of wear, a squire had to be engaged permanently.

The old belief that full armour was so heavy that the knight had to be lifted on to his horse and could not rise unaided if he fell is not true. It was really little heavier than the full kit of a soldier in the First World War.

When a knight, helped by his squire, dressed for battle, he first put on a close-fitting shirt, short breeches and hose, then his *aketon*, a quilted coat worn underneath the armour. This

was followed by a mail shirt called either a *hauberk* or *byrnie* and over that went the breast plate. His knee guards were called *poleyns* and on his feet he wore *sabatons* which had overlapping horizontal metal plates. Finally the plumed helmet was placed over his head and with the visor lowered he was ready for combat – a fearsome sight indeed! He did not, however, feel very fearsome. Indeed, after a short time, the gallant knight usually felt extremely hot because of the lack of ventilation. Impregnable to sword thrusts his greatest danger was that of suffocation.

There was an attempt in the nineteenth century to reconstruct that fabled age of chivalry when knights were bold and spent their time rescuing damsels in distress, or jousting with each other in tournaments.

The Victorians were brought up on tales of King Arthur and his shining knights of the Round Table, of fairy castles and readings of Scott's *Ivanhoe*. Men longed to be gallant knights battling in tournaments; girls dreamed of being Queens of Beauty handing their scarves to chosen champions for them to wear on the ends of their lances. And a young aristocrat named Archibald Montgomerie decided that, for one glorious day at least, all this was going to be possible.

Archibald was furious with the decision of the Government that the young Victoria was to be crowned queen with a minimum of pomp and ceremony. The country was having a bout of economy at the time on account of some difficulties with the balance of payments (yes, just like modern times!) and it had been decided that many of the ceremonies which had been carried out on similar occasions for the past six centuries should be abolished.

One such ceremony was the appearance at the Royal

A First Book of Antiques

Banquet in Westminster Hall of the Sovereign's Champion. He was a knight in full armour who rode up to the doors and threw down his gauntlet as a challenge to anyone who opposed the sovereign's claim to the throne.

This event had not always been successful in the past. In 1689 at the coronation of William and Mary, as the Champion flung his gauntlet to the ground, an old woman appeared from among the onlookers, picked up the gauntlet, and with a harsh cackle like that of one of the witches in *Macbeth*, vanished into the crowd. Even earlier, at the coronation of James II in 1685, the Champion had flung the gauntlet with such force and enthusiasm that he had followed it with himself, and lay on the ground, too winded to rise immediately. The King had laughed.

In view of all this and bothered as his Government was by the Chartists and by crowds of unemployed weavers demanding bread and work, the Prime Minister in 1838, Viscount Melbourne, decided that the age of chivalry was dead – and, with it, the Sovereign's Champion.

Archibald Montgomerie made up his mind that the romantic glory of the past should not die, and immediately the coronation was over he announced his plans for holding a medieval tournament at Eglinton Castle, which stood in Ayrshire, about thirty miles from Glasgow. Young bloods, eager for new thrills, clamoured to become knights, and all London society was eager to know who would be Queen of Beauty.

Archibald chose a small band of young men for training in the forgotten art of jousting. The difficult part, they soon found, was getting the horses to run the length of the wooden fence on each side of which two fully-armoured knights were to ride towards each other tilting their lances. The armour, horses and weapons cost £500 per person, the armour having to be specially made. It was found that the human old suits in British museums were too small; the race had increased in stature since the Middle Ages.

The great day was to be August 28, 1839, and it was hoped that at least 1,500 people would apply for tickets; in fact there were 10,000 applications, and even this was nothing compared with the actual number who attended. When the day came it was estimated that there must have been 100,000 spectators crowding the stands, the trees and the banks of the river.

Most of them were to regret having come.

The morning was cool and cloudy, and the rain – which nobody had thought about because there were no weather forecasts in those days – had already started when the vast crowds were jamming the narrow road that led to Irvine, the nearest town 2½ miles from the castle. So thick were the coaches that many people had to get out and walk.

The official procession was three hours late in leaving the castle where chaos reigned. The lovely Lady Seymour, who after much argument and intrigue, had been selected as Queen of Beauty, was to have driven round the arena in an open carriage. But the rain caused this to be cancelled and nobody saw her.

The royal box and all the grandstands were flooded at an early stage as the rainfall became a typical Ayrshire torrent, and a gale began.

The ceremony of proclaiming a challenge, of the heralds announcing the rules of the tournament and the identities of the knights, had to be cancelled. And in the pouring rain and

A First Book of Antiques

cold wind the knights missed each other as their horses slid in the mud. The banquet and costume ball were cancelled because the huge marquee in which they were to be held had become a waterlogged, gale-swept ruin.

Many people had sent their carriages away, and as the afternoon's dismal events were cut short, they now found themselves marooned. Tens of thousands of soaked visitors struggled back along the muddy road from the castle; country yokels mixed with rich guests clothed in medieval dress that had taken weeks to prepare. Many spent that night huddled in cowsheds. The knights wandered back to the castle, their expensive armour already rusting.

When Archibald came to count the cost of his dream he found that the family fortunes were almost ruined. If the age of knights in armour were not already dead it was truly laid to rest that rainy day in Ayrshire.

Suits of armour can be seen in most museums, but for a good idea of what the figures wearing them looked like it is useful to visit some of our cathedrals and see the recumbent figures of stone or marble, wearing full attire.

Armour is not so easy to buy today, but the various parts can still be found with patient searching.

FURTHER READING

Armour and Weapons by Paul Martin (Herbert Jenkins)
Armour by J. F. Hayward (Victoria & Albert Museum)

2
Daggers

Daggers might be said to be almost as old as a cave man's stone club. When a primitive man first stabbed another with a long piece of pointed slate he was using the first dagger. As a true military weapon, however, it was not until the middle of the thirteenth century that it officially came into use.

Daggers vary immensely, some are very short, some so long that is is difficult to distinguish them from swords. In the seventeenth century some daggers were actually made by cutting down a broadsword.

In the early nineteenth century in Scotland there was a romantic revival of the ornamental dagger, and many were made with elaborate decoration and carried in silver-mounted sheaths. The novelist Sir Walter Scott was one of the people behind this revival. An earlier Scottish dagger was the dirk, which had a wide blade and a carved wooden handle.

One very interesting type made in the seventeenth and eighteenth centuries was the gunners' stiletto. This had a long blade on one side of which was engraved a series of numbers and lines which enabled the gunner to measure the bore of a gun barrel and then calculate the correct weight of shot required.

In the East, too, daggers were popular. The Indians made *katars*; one type of these opens out to form a three-pronged blade. *Jambaias* are Arabian daggers with a double-edged blade. Another kind made by the Arabs is the *khanjar* and has a double, curved blade and a hilt that is more like a pistol butt. Some khanjars have grips of precious jade inset with jewels. From Afghanistan comes the Khyber dagger called the *kard* which has a special point made for piercing chain mail.

But one of the most famous of all is a plain variety that originated in America and was called the 'Bowie Knife'.

James Bowie was born in Kentucky in the 1790s and when he grew up he owned a sugar mill in partnership with his brother Rezin. The story goes that he became involved in a fight with a man whom he killed by stabbing with an old file, the only weapon to hand at the time. After this Bowie is said to have taken the file to a blacksmith who made it into a knife with a single edge and a curved point.

Bowie was described by a friend as being a man who 'never used profane language, always respected women and loved children and animals. He never picked a quarrel with anybody.' Despite these gentlemanly qualities other people seemed often to pick quarrels with him, and in some of these fights his knife came in very handy.

When Bowie went prospecting for gold he was involved in several battles with Indians. These exploits led to many tales being told about him and he eventually became a hero of fiction. In the 1830s he joined what was already a lost cause: the fight for the independence of the State of Texas, and he was besieged in the fortress called the Alamo in 1836 when the place was attacked by hundreds of Mexican soldiers.

According to legend, Bowie died fighting, his famous

Daggers

knife in hand. But the reality is less romantic: he was very ill with pneumonia when the Mexicans made the last assault that captured the fortress, and he was killed in his bed.

He made his mark in history with the invention of his dagger which soon became very popular on the wild American frontier. So popular in fact, that cutlers in Sheffield began making them to export to America. Some of both the English and American ones can still be found, and are often engraved.

FURTHER READING

Daggers and Swords by Frederick Wilkinson (Ward Lock)
Swords and Daggers by J. F. Hayward (Victoria & Albert Museum)
Daggers & Fighting Knives of the Western World by Harold L. Peterson (Herbert Jenkins)

3
Flint-lock Pistols and other Firearms

THE thunder of hoofs pounding the turf, a wild shouting of commands and the line of cavalry charges recklessly towards the foe – a row of men crouching on one knee, with long, fearsome pikes held out firmly in front of them. Farther back the massed ranks of men armed with swords await the onslaught.

Nearer, nearer – then at an order from the captain the horses wheel, gallop along the row of pikemen; their riders raise long-barrelled pistols and pull the triggers. Steel strikes flint, spark ignites powder, and a steel ball, small but deadly, flames from each barrel.

Such was the first action in many battles of the sixteenth century.

The aim of those flint-lock pistols was uncertain and the recoil did not help. Sometimes the attackers would be lucky and the pikemen would be broken by the volley. Once the cavalry captain saw that this had happened he would order his men to turn their horses again, sheathe the smoking pistols which could not be used again until they had been reprimed with powder and another ball rammed into the barrel, and charge into the enemy infantry, slashing about them with drawn swords. If the pikemen had not broken, then the cavalry would retire and make way for either another wave of horsemen with flint-locks or an attack with swords by their own infantry.

The guns did little real damage and casualties were usually very light. Undoubtedly they frightened more than they hurt – and the men who fired them were often as scared as the enemy!

Any miscalculation in measuring the amount of powder could easily cause the gun to burst. An additional danger was that cunning powder suppliers sometimes put coal-dust into the mixture in place of saltpetre, one of the vital elements of gunpowder. The usual advice to those who owned guns was to test the powder by tasting it. The taste should be sharp if it contained the right amounts of saltpetre, charcoal and sulphur. There are no records of the possible harm to the tasters caused by this practice!

The principle of the flint-lock was probably brought to Europe from Japan by Portuguese navigators who must have seen the Japanese using flint and steel lighters to ignite their tobacco pipes.

The Chinese had invented gunpowder long ago but used it only for fireworks; the Japanese invented the flint-lock but used it only for their pipes. It was left to the European white to use both inventions to kill his own kind.

Before the flint-lock Europeans had to rely on the wheel-lock, a less efficient weapon which worked on the principle of stone rubbing against metal. One type of wheel-lock was the *arquebus* or *harquebus*. This was fired from a fixed rest and had to be primed and set up every time an advance was made.

In 1471 Edward IV landed at Ravenscar, on the Yorkshire coast, with 300 Flemish mercenaries armed with what were described as 'hand gonnes'. These were probably a type with a rough wooden shaft and a touch-hole containing powder on top of the breech. A naked flame was necessary to ignite the powder and blow the lead or copper ball along the barrel. The snag about this was the impossibility of surprise at night because the flame revealed the soldier's position and the fact that he was about to attack. Also, if it was windy, the powder was likely to be blown away.

At a later stage the touch-hole was placed at the side, which gave some protection from the wind, but the invention of the wheel-lock was a great step forward since it did away with the cumbersome business of having to use a flame to ignite powder exposed to the elements. The wheel-lock also enabled one to sneak up on the enemy at night. The flint-lock was a still greater advance.

In the early years of these weapons in the fifteenth century, it was common practice to fire arrows from the guns until someone found that metal balls were cheaper and more plentiful. The balls were always bought by the pound weight. Usually ten or twelve weighed 1 lb.

Guns firing balls which penetrated armour were regarded as very unsporting weapons. They were even denounced as 'un-Christian!' One can imagine the conservative-minded old soldiers of the fifteenth century saying, 'Bows and arrows were good enough for my father. We don't need these devilish newfangled contraptions!' Perhaps somebody even said, 'If everybody had one of these fearsome weapons then war would become too destructive to be allowed!'

The early hand guns used by men on horseback made such a noise, spitting fire and smoke, that they earned the name of 'dragons', and that was how cavalry came to be called 'dragoons'.

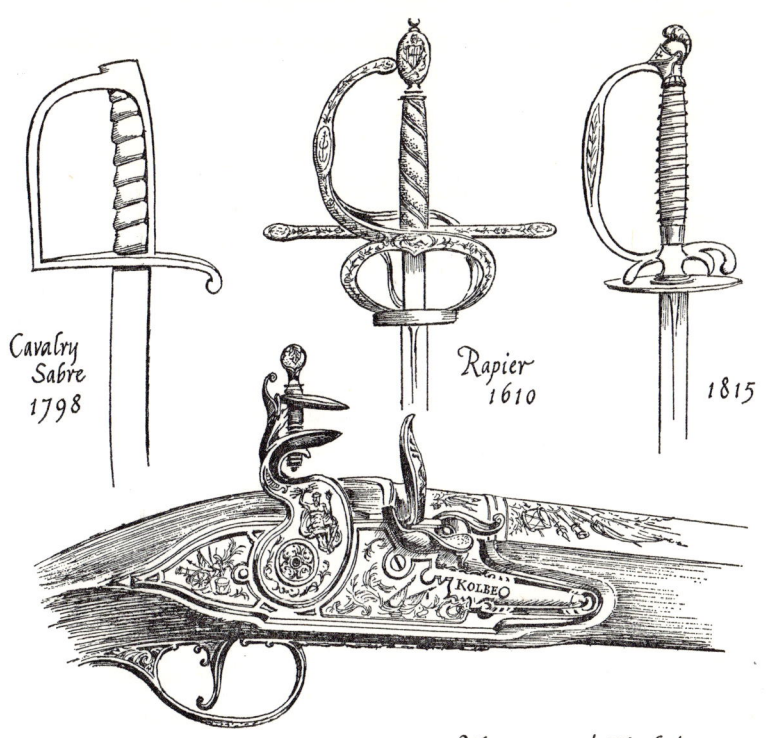

Cavalry Sabre 1798

Rapier 1610

1815

Silver-mounted Flintlock gun c. 1735

In 1690 the British army was equipped with flint-locks called 'Brown Besses' because of the browning applied to prevent rust. Naval officers were issued with brass-barrelled pistols on the grounds that brass did not rust at sea so easily as steel.

One type of antique firearm which is always popular with collectors is the duelling pistol. It is also one of the most decorative. It first appeared in 1760, and in 1777 the *Code Duello* laid down rules that such pistols should be 9 to 10 inches in length, firing very light balls of which there were

A First Book of Antiques

forty-eight to the pound. These weapons had to have a high standard of accuracy and reliability, and the grip had to be specially designed. Achieving the balance was an art in itself.

Special cases were made for them, usually of mahogany or oak and lined with Irish baize. The pistols and cases were carved and decorated, some very beautifully. A duelling pistol is always more valuable if it can be found complete with case.

During the American War of Independence (1775–83) there was a need for light-weight guns that could be carried easily, and so the Kentucky Rifle was designed with a 42-inch barrel firing three balls to the pound. Its stock was of maple wood, often carved.

Another gun popular with collectors is the Colt, invented by Samuel Colt, an American, who used the principle of the revolving cylinder which contained several bullets (hence the name "revolver"). The cylinder brought one bullet at a time to its place in the barrel ready for firing.

Colt believed he was the first to use this idea but when he visited England in 1835 he found that it was quite well known already, though his weapon proved in practice to be superior to anything then in use.

In 1846, when the U.S.A. was at war with Mexico and everybody wanted revolvers, Samuel Colt went into business in a big way. The guns which he made in America are all marked 'New York'. In 1851 he came to England and started a factory at Pimlico. The guns made there are marked on the barrel 'Address Colt, London'.

Some antique dealers specialize entirely in old guns, while others just devote one part of their business to them. Sometimes you will find that gunsmiths keep one part of their counter for antique firearms which they sell as a sideline.

Flint-lock Pistols and other Firearms

If you do buy an antique gun be very careful about operating any part of it until you have sufficient knowledge. Such actions as 'snapping the flint' can easily damage any part which may have been weakened by the years. It is useful to be able to tell whether a weapon has been re-finished, whether a new lock has been fitted or the stock repaired. Guns, unlike the majority of antiques, have moving parts which wear out, and replacements can reduce their value. Cleaning and repairing old guns has to be done very carefully. There is no reason why, to some extent, you should not learn to do this yourself. There are several very useful books on the subject.

Very little is published in Britain in the way of periodicals on antique fire-arms, but there are quite a number of American magazines which you can see on the bookstalls here.

FURTHER READING

Antique Firearms by Ron Lister (Herbert Jenkins)
(A very useful book about how to clean and repair guns)
Gun Collecting by G. Boothroyd (Mayflower Paperback)
Antique Pistol Collecting by R. Andrews and J. Frith (Holland Press)

4
Swords

AMONG all the weapons with which man has ever fought, the sword is one of the oldest.

Sculptures and paintings found in Egypt show swords shaped like a sickle in use as long ago as 3000 B.C.; and ancient Greek vases have pictures of warriors wielding swords that are curved with the cutting edge on the inside, like the much later *kukri* of the Ghurkas.

The Greeks used their swords chiefly for slashing, but the Roman *gladius*, a shorter type with a hilt of bronze, alabaster, or sometimes ivory from African elephants, was really a stabbing weapon. The Roman soldier carried his gladius on his right side where its short length made it convenient for the quick and easy draw.

Imagine a centurion in Julius Caesar's 10th Legion, which invaded Britain. He is practising on the deck of the galley carrying the armoured legionaries across the Channel on that fateful day in 55 B.C. Perhaps his name is Septimus Aurelius. He stands there with his back to the receding coast of Gaul; ahead of him are the tall white cliffs on which stand line after line of Britons in war-paint waiting to defend their island which Septimus knows as *Ultima Thule*, the ultimate land on the fringes of the known world.

'*Io triumphe!*' Septimus shouts, and swift as lightning he whips his gladius from his belt, showing his well-known skill

Swords

as the 'quickest draw' in the west of the Empire. Not that his speed helped Septimus much when some time later he stumbled through the shallow water towards the beach, waving his gladius as the screaming, savage Britons bore down on him in their war chariots, cutting down the men from Rome as they struggled in the water, weighed down by their armour and heavy shields.

But the power of the legions prevailed in the end. As Septimus lay in the water, cursing and nursing his wounds, the standard bearer of the 10th Legion reached the top of the cliff, gladius in one hand, standard in the other, and planted the eagles of Rome on the soil of Britain.

From then onwards the short stabbing swords carved their way north until their bearers reached the borders of Scotland where Hadrian ordered the wall that carries his name to be built.

During the centuries of occupation that followed, the Britons bore arms under Roman officers and learned to handle the gladius. Later, when the legions withdrew to guard the distant walls of a crumbling empire, leaving the islanders to their freedom and independence, the Britons designed their own swords, but for many centuries afterwards they remained very similar to the gladius.

It was with this type of weapon that the Saxon Harold met the invading Normans at Hastings in 1066, and the Normans themselves having – like the Britons – been subject peoples of Rome, carried similar swords. Their cavalry used a longer slashing sword with a double edge, and this was descended from the *spatha* which had been used by Roman cavalry. As Britain settled down under Norman occupation, swords

A First Book of Antiques

became longer, and by the end of the thirteenth century were from 45 inches to 55 inches in length.

It was in the sixteenth century that swords began to be worn as part of civilian dress. This practice started in Spain where the young bloods who could swagger about carrying finely-decorated Toledo blades were the envy of their friends.

The best blades were made in Toledo and Valencia in Spain, though craftsmen of Milan in Italy were also held in high repute. It was probably about 1530 when Spain produced the rapier, a civilian weapon made of the finest steel and often beautifully decorated. She brought both this and the ornamental dress sword to a fine peak of decoration; and some of them, with their hilts encrusted with silver work or studded with jewels, are superb creations.

In old pictures of Spaniards fencing with rapiers, men are sometimes shown with a glove on the left hand, or a cloak wrapped round the left arm. The cloak was employed as a kind of shield with which to parry an opponent's thrust; the glove, always mailed, was used to grasp his sword.

The sixteenth century also saw the development of a very different sword from the light, flickering rapier: the great two-handed sword. This was very popular in Northern Europe among the muscular descendants of the Vikings. It was about 6 feet in length and was whirled round and round the head, slashing anyone foolish enough to get within range. In Scotland it was called the cláidheam-mor, a name later anglicized as claymore.

There were also the basket-hilted swords which appeared at this time in Germany. The cage or basket of metal bars protected the hand.

Swords

By the end of the seventeenth century there was a reversion to something like the Roman gladius; a new type of short sword about 30 inches long. This often had a finely decorated hilt, and is very popular with collectors today.

British infantrymen carried swords until 1786, when they were officially withdrawn, though officers continued to carry the small-sword. An order of 1796 stated that these must be straight-bladed with hilts of brass. Cavalry also abandoned swords when later weapons made them useless.

Generals are often accused of thinking in terms of the last war rather than the one being fought, and it was only in 1908 that a committee of the British army approved what was considered to be the best cavalry sword ever designed. Six years later came the First World War with machine-guns and tanks which made this 'finest of cavalry swords' as out of date as the bow and arrow.

Swords from the East are as much valued by collectors as are European ones, especially the Indian *tulwars* with their fine silver and gold decoration. The blades of these vary greatly, some being only 1 inch wide while others may be as much as 4 inches. They are usually curved and were carried in decorated scabbards. Turkish and Persian blades, too, are generally curved. This is in fact typical of Eastern swords and seems to have been so since the early seventeenth century. Some of the most valuable Turkish and Persian ones have verses from the Koran engraved on the blades.

One of the commonest and most inexpensive swords to collect is the Ghurka *kukri*, but the plain and unornamented ones are of little value. The best are those in fine sheaths with silver decoration.

From south-east Asia comes the *kris* which probably

A First Book of Antiques

originated in Java. This varies according to the country of manufacture. Sometimes the blade is straight, sometimes wavy. China did not produce swords of any real interest other than the great two-handed executioner's swords with wide curved blades and hilts of steel or brass.

Japanese swords are very different, however; they are probably the most ornate in the world. Almost all date from before 1876 when the carrying of them was forbidden. The Samurai warrior practically worshipped his sword and passed it on with respect from one generation to another. It was created with loving care by the most highly skilled craftsmen who were proud of their work and often marked the sword with their name and the date of manufacture, a convenient habit not followed by makers in many other countries.

If one is to collect swords, one must first make a careful study of the different styles and periods. A good way to begin is to look at items in museums; after that a visit to an auction room provides a good chance of actually handling one; it is useful to get to know the feel of a sword and its scabbard, and to examine the decoration from every angle.

Feel, look – and bear in mind that with this particular antique there is no guide to prices; they vary too much.

FURTHER READING

The Sword in the age of Chivalry by Ewart Oakeshott (Lutterworth Press)

Swords & Daggers by J. F. Hayward (Victoria & Albert Museum)

5
Chippendale and his Furniture

ALMOST every antique shop, auction room and antiques fair has some items of furniture described as 'Chippendale' or 'Chippendale style', but if Thomas Chippendale had really made all the furniture so labelled he would have had to have as many hands as an octopus besides living about twice the normal human span.

The difficult thing about collecting any British furniture is that our makers, unlike the French, did not generally sign their work; and there was no system, such as hallmarks on silver, by which furniture was marked.

How, then, do you know that Chippendale furniture is really Chippendale and not Sheraton, Hepplewhite, Adam, or anything else? The answer is that you have to study the style of the masters and the fashions of the periods, so that in time you will be able to say that this chair or that cabinet is made in one of the designs produced by Chippendale and might just possibly have been created by the great man himself, though in most cases this is unlikely and often impossible to tell.

Thomas Chippendale was born in Otley, Yorkshire, in 1718. This turned out to be a fortunate place for him to live as it is only a few miles from Harewood House, historic home of the Lascelles family who were to set him on the road to fame.

At an early age Thomas was apprenticed to a cabinet

A First Book of Antiques

maker, and one of the notable things he made in that youthful period was a very elaborate dolls' house in mahogany which can be seen today at Nostell Priory, in Yorkshire. It is one object which we can be certain was made with his own hands. Soon he was employed in making furniture for Harewood House out of oak grown on the estate, and it was then that the family took an interest in him. There is little doubt that, recognizing his genius, they paid for him to go to London and establish his own furniture business.

Once settled in St. Martin's Lane he began to prepare a book of furniture designs. This unique work was called the *Gentleman and Cabinet-Maker's Director*, contained 150 entirely new designs and took two years to set out. Thomas, who was apparently a firm believer in the power of advertising, spread the word of his forthcoming book among the upper classes who were likely customers for furniture.

The *Director* was the first really complete pattern book of furniture design to become available to everyone who could afford a copy. Within a few years it was recognized as a standard reference book for wood-workers, enabling even those in remote parts of the provinces to copy new fashions and have them ready for sale within a short time after they appeared. Previously this involved a time lag of several years.

A person described as a genius is often so partly because he knows how to use other people's brains, and Thomas was no exception. He employed two very talented designers to create most of his drawings in the book but their names do not appear anywhere; and it was published under the name of Chippendale.

When the famous book finally came out it was sold at £2 8s 6d per copy, and in those days that was a vast sum indeed. Thomas was a clever psychologist and reasoned that the rich would not be impressed by anything sold at a reasonable price, but if it was very expensive they would feel that it was something rare and exclusive which they must have. The idea worked: the book sold in great numbers.

Clever ideas are soon copied and it was not long before competitors were producing their own pattern books on similar lines. But they never equalled the sales of the *Director*, which was a remarkable publication.

Until that time there were two basic themes in furniture design in Britain. The first was copied from the Chinese and was called *chinoiserie*. This goes back to the seventeenth century when Europe was opening up the eastern sea routes to the fabulous land known as 'Cathay' and became fascinated by Chinese silks, porcelains and engravings of architecture. Chinoiserie is often found in European porcelain and pottery, and in jewellery and glassware.

In furniture chinoiserie designs made particular use of pagoda-like shapes and in the Victoria and Albert Museum there is a superb Chippendale bedstead surmounted by a pagoda top. The top rails of chairs are often carved in this shape, and his tables and chairs have clustered legs in imitation of bamboo.

Chinoiserie was to be found all over Europe but the other style, Gothic, was peculiar to Britain. No other country seemed really to care for it.

There was a craze among the rich in eighteenth-century Britain for building their mansions in the form of sham castles with battlements and arches, and these Gothic elements were transferred to furniture design along with tracery and pinnacles copied from cathedrals,

Thomas Chippendale created a revolution in mahogany furniture by fusing these two themes into a style which was lighter and more graceful than the heavy Georgian designs then in vogue. One of the most important features of his style is the lattice work applied to the doors of cabinets, the backs of chairs and beds, and the edges of tables. The chairs often have curved splats with the line of the top rail broken or curved.

In the *Director* there is a new design for a richly carved dressing-table which was to become very popular. It had a recessed front with drawers flanked by two sets of cabriole legs and surmounted by a mirror draped with material.

Chippendale's bookcases were often extremely large and were used in libraries in place of fitted shelves. His commodes were highly ornamented and with these he allowed a fondness for French styling to creep in.

Some of his finest furniture went into the two houses of the actor-manager, David Garrick, in Adelphi Terrace, London and Hampton-on-Thames. Examples of this can be seen today in the Victoria and Albert Museum.

The gentry were ready for something new and took eagerly to Chippendale's designs. Commissions poured in and his business expanded to become the foremost in the country. Soon other makers began to imitate him and vast quantities of furniture in the Chippendale style were turned out. Much of this was made by first-class craftsmen whose pieces are well worth collecting; particularly in view of the virtual impossibility of knowing which were made by Thomas himself.

In later years he made return visits to Harewood House to create more masterpieces there in collaboration with the

Chippendale and his Furniture

famous architect and designer Robert Adam. In gratitude for the help which the Lascelles family had given him he produced some of his finest work for Harewood and we can see this there today and know that it, at least, was formed by the hands of Thomas Chippendale.

The best way to become acquainted with the Chippendale style, and thus be better able to recognize the genuine article, is to study examples either at Harewood or in the Victoria and Albert Museum.

It is a remarkable fact that his firm was never among the largest in Britain. He rarely employed more than about 20 craftsmen although there were firms which employed 200 and even, in a few cases, 300. Nevertheless he seemed to acquire the best contracts from the richest and most famous people.

It was quality on which Thomas Chippendale concentrated his efforts, not quantity, and it is his name which time has immortalized in the realm of British furniture.

FURTHER READING

Chippendale Furniture by Anthony Coleridge (Faber & Faber)
Old English Furniture by Hampden Gordon (John Murray Paperback)

6
The Age of Walnut

For ten years, from 1649 to 1659, the killjoy shadow of Puritanism lay over England. Pleasure and merry-making were frowned upon. To the harsh Puritan soul life was too serious for fun – certainly too serious to permit foolish extravagance in the design of furniture.

When Puritans gathered in their comfortless homes it was to sit on their hard chairs of good English oak. There was a stern economy in the use to which items of furniture were put. A chest, for example, would also serve as a table.

The styles of oaken furniture were heavy and practical. The pieces were built to last for many generations. Then came the end of the Cromwellian period and the restoration of the monarchy in 1660; and the reaction against the drabness of those ten years was symbolized by a new fashion in furniture – this time in the lighter material of walnut. There was an outburst of gaiety, a desire for brightening surroundings with new styles and designs, and the new king, having spent most of his life on the Continent, brought with him new ideas and a wave of experimentation in art and fashion. As Pepys wrote in his *Diary*, 'All the world's in a merry mood.'

Much furniture in the mansions of the rich had been destroyed in the Civil War, and in 1666 vast stocks were wiped out in the Great Fire of London. The losses caused by both

Windsor
18th Century

William & Mary
1690

Chippendale
Ribbon-backed
1760

Hepplewhite
1775

Corner bergère
Louis XV style

A First Book of Antiques

these events had to be made good and the furniture makers were thus stimulated to increase their output. New factories sprang up, designers and craftsmen poured in from France and Holland. Ornamentation, no longer frowned upon, was reinstated – and walnut was found to suit the new mood admirably.

There was plenty of it. The forests of walnut planted in the reign of Elizabeth were now mature. Its pleasant colouring and the uniformity of its texture gave walnut advantages over oak, which always had a tendency to swell or shrink under certain conditions. The wood was easy to use as a veneer on yellow deal, or the solid wood could be cut and worked into artistic shapes. Burrs from protuberances at the base of the trunk provided a finely mottled grain, and by cutting obliquely across the branches the type of veneer known as 'oyster shell' could be obtained.

After a while the English walnut proved insufficient and foreign species were imported. The Italian walnut gave a close-grained texture with dark streaks, which was superb for decorative purposes. The French was straight-grained and a lighter grey colour. From Virginia came the dark, so-called black walnut free from the worm that troubled the English variety.

The new class of rich merchants which was springing up as the trading routes to the Eastern world developed, had money to spend on furniture and the designers began to provide a variety of items for special purposes. Tables were now for use as tables only. Day beds became fashionable, and a new craze for collecting china led to the production of the china cabinet with glass doors. Now that games were no longer frowned upon, the new age of greater laxity deman-

The Age of Walnut

ded tables for cards and for draughts and chess. Literacy became more widespread. People began to read and write more and so bookcases and writing-tables called escritoires were made.

The legs of furniture took on new shapes: from Portugal came the spiral twist, and from France the cabriole leg, like a rather elongated pear. Previously cross-pieces known as 'stretchers' had reinforced the legs, but by the time of William and Mary (1689–1702) these had been abandoned and the beautiful cabriole legs stood by themselves ending in a club or ball-and-claw foot.

Chair backs became higher and more curved to give better support and greater comfort. Elegant stools appeared; and with the arrival in 1685 of Huguenot refugees bringing new skills, came a fashion for fine upholstery.

One of the most spectacular of the new ideas was floral marquetry for hall stands, small tables and the front panels of the long-case (grandfather) clocks, which were made just as the Age of Walnut started.

Veneering became very popular. This custom had begun on the Continent, and consisted of cutting very thin layers of decorative woods and gluing them to the surface of the base wood. The Dutch craftsmen had brought to a high pitch of skill the fine art of piecing together the delicate patterns of different woods. The elm, the yew and the olive were all very suitable materials for veneering, as well as walnut. Designs using figures of birds and flowers which originated with the Flemish designers were much in demand.

Another fashion was lacquering, or 'japanning' as it was sometimes called because of its origin. In the East it consisted of painting on to the wood the resin, or lacquer, of a tree

A First Book of Antiques

called the *Rhus vernicifera,* and allowing each layer to dry before applying another. Many layers were used until a considerable thickness was built up which could then be painted or decorated with designs in gold leaf. Europeans could not make the true lacquer because the tree did not grow in the West; but a number of substitute methods were invented.

Yet another method of decorating walnut was the use of gesso. This came into fashion in the late 1690s. Like lacquering it involved a building up of layer after layer of substance, in this case a mixture of whiting and parchment size. A pattern was then made in relief by cutting away the background. This was burnished, but quite often the colouring tended to fade with time. The method was at its most successful when gold leaf was used.

Cane seats are another feature of the walnut period. They were introduced at the same time as loose cushions, in themselves a symptom of the demand for comfort as Britain emerged from Puritanism and moved into the eighteenth century.

The sixty glorious years of the Age of Walnut spanned the following reigns which give their names to the various styles:

Charles II (1660–85) including the brief reign of James II (1685–88).

William and Mary (1689–1702), a period characterized by a settling down to quieter styles after the gaiety of the immediate post-Puritan period.

Queen Anne (1702–14), noted especially for the hooped backs and curved seat frames of chairs.

George I (1714–27) and George II (1727–1760). These two constitute the Georgian period.

The Age of Walnut

London, already one of the world's biggest cities, had a population of about 500,000 and it had become a major centre of furniture production in which there was a vast export trade. Although walnut is less durable than oak it is surprising what a large quantity has managed to survive and can still be found.

FURTHER READING

Old English Furniture by Hampden Gordon (John Murray)
The Complete Encyclopaedia of Antiques (The Connoisseur)
   See pages 243 to 245.
English Period Furniture by Charles H. Hayward (Evans Bros)
Going for a Song by Arthur Negus (B.B.C. Publications)

7
Some more Furniture

WE HAVE already dealt with the furniture of Chippendale and with the wide range of items produced during the Age of Walnut; and to describe the whole vast subject of antique furniture would need a very large book indeed. However, the other main types for which collectors are always on the look out are those of Hepplewhite, Sheraton, Adam, and Louis XIV.

The designer of the first of these, George Hepplewhite, never knew the fame which his designs brought him for he died too soon. Nothing much is known about his early career; we do not even know for certain when he was born, only that he died in 1786 leaving behind him a book entitled *The Cabinet-Maker and Upholsterers' Guide*. This work, soon to be as famous as had been Chippendale's *Director*, was only in manuscript form when the author died. His wife published it two years later and its designs were quickly copied and brought considerable prosperity to the small furniture business which Hepplewhite had owned. Because of his death he himself made very little furniture in the Hepplewhite style.

One of the most obvious characteristics of Hepplewhite furniture is the oval or shield-like shape of the backs of chairs. These backs are always suspended between the uprights at each side and never touch the rail of the seat. Once you have seen a chair like this it is always a useful way to recognize the

Some more Furniture

true Hepplewhite style. A typical form of his decoration is carving in the shape of wheat ears, or a string of husks; and an almost certain sign is a plume-of-feathers design in the chair back. Another is the square leg which always tapers on the inside.

The fashion which Chippendale had started of publishing a pattern book was now quite common, and it was only five years after Hepplewhite's death that Thomas Sheraton produced his *Cabinet-Maker and Upholsterers' Drawing Book*.

Sheraton was a curious character. He was born about 1750 and began his career, not in the furniture trade, but as a Baptist preacher. He seems to have been of a very narrow Puritan outlook. Shortly after the publication of his book he was described by a friend as, 'dwelling in an obscure back street and looking very worn out in a threadbare black coat.'

Why he turned from preaching to furniture design no one knows, but he was evidently a fine draughtsman and also had a very high opinion of his own talents as an artist, besides an equally low opinion of the talents of others. Sheraton referred to Chippendale and Hepplewhite with a sneer as, 'old-fashioned compared with the new and better style'. By new and better style he meant, of course, his own designs.

Unlike the other designers, he never seems to have owned a business. That he produced any furniture himself is doubtful, and he died in poverty in 1806.

His designs show a great deal of japanned and inlaid work. The lines that he favoured were, in accordance with his Puritan preaching, straight and severe, avoiding the gentle curves of Chippendale and Hepplewhite. Sheraton pioneered the straight-back chair and made much use of satin-wood for inlays.

A First Book of Antiques

He was one of the four great designers of English furniture who all lived and worked during the last half of the eighteenth century: Chippendale, Hepplewhite, Sheraton and – giant of them all – Robert Adam.

Robert Adam did not actually make furniture at all; he was an architect, but his influence on furniture design proved to be immense. He spent his early life travelling in France and Italy, coming to London about 1760 when he joined with his brother James in founding a business known afterwards as 'The Adelphi'.

Adam designed and decorated famous country mansions including the Earl of Mansfield's Kenwood, Syon House for the Duke of Northumberland, and Harewood House for which he engaged Thomas Chippendale to design the furniture. He believed that the furnishings of a house should match its architecture. He brought from the Continent the classical art form which he tried – and very often succeeded – to transplant from sunnier skies to the damper and greyer climate of Britain.

His furniture was part of his grand design. An Adam mantelpiece once seen is easily recognized again. It has a straight, classical outline with slender columns and is inset with plaques of Greek or Roman figures. He favoured huge wall mirrors in narrow frames, and lamps on tall gilt tripods. His chairs are usually painted and have straight slim backs. The tables are coloured in gold and white, and decorated with Wedgwood medallions designed by the artist Flaxman.

In the typical Adam house there are beautiful painted ceilings and moulded friezes, and often a great deal of decoration which looks like wood but is really a composition of resin, whiting and size very cleverly moulded together.

Some more Furniture

The legacy of Robert Adam is not only his influence on furniture design but the many stately homes of England which he designed and which still remain for us to visit today.

The glory of Continental furniture, some would say of all furniture, is that produced during the reign of Louis XIV of France, the 'Sun King' as he is often called.

Louis came to the throne at the age of five and had an immensely long reign, from 1643 to 1715. He became virtually a dictator, making France powerful and feared, and indulging in wars of aggression which eventually ruined the nation and destroyed much that he had built. Military defeat and economic collapse could not, however, extinguish the work that had been done in literature and design during his reign.

In 1662 he inspired the setting up of the *Manufacture de Meubles de la Couronne* at Gobelins. Through this organization the arts were assured of royal patronage. It gathered together a glittering galaxy of artistic talent, both French and foreign, and encouraged the creation of great works of art and the development of new standards of taste and design. One of the first tasks which it undertook was the decoration and furnishing of the King's new palace at Versailles; and it was here that André Charles Boulle, one of Europe's greatest masters of furniture design, had his workshops. He produced some of the most elaborate and beautiful furniture, often ornamented with plaques of Sèvres porcelain and Wedgwood Jasper.

Unlike the makers of English furniture the French invariably signed their work, though sometimes it is necessary to get an expert to take up part of the upholstery to find the signature, but at least it is certain proof of the age of the piece and its origin.

In honour of the King quite a lot of Louis XIV furniture has the emblem of the sun's rays worked into its decoration. The *fleur de lys* too, was commonly used.

Furniture of this kind is naturally very expensive, and as an investment it has been described as second only to paintings.

The styles dealt with in this chapter are only a few in the whole wide range of antique furniture. There are also the French periods of Louis XV and XVI, the Age of Oak and the Age of Mahogany, Victorian, and many others.

When buying any antique furniture it is essential to note whether there are signs that it may have been cut down from a larger piece, thus reducing its value. Furniture of the past which has come from the great houses of the rich was often made large to fit big high-ceilinged rooms, whereas today because most people live in relatively small homes the demand is for much smaller items. Unscrupulous fakers sometimes cut a large chest of drawers in half. When this happens the handles usually have to be moved to maintain the balance, so look out for marks showing where the handles may have been. Always look at the drawer runners to see if they show signs of the wear that comes with years of use.

FURTHER READING

French Royal Furniture by Pierre Verlet (Barrie & Rockliffe)
Adam & Hepplewhite Furniture by Clifford Musgrave (Faber & Faber)
Sheraton Furniture by Ralph Fastnedge (Faber & Faber)
Plain Man's Guide to Second-Hand Furniture by Frank Davis (Michael Joseph)
Old English Furniture by Hampden Gordon (John Murray Paperback)

8

Horse Brasses

HORSE brasses are among the most plentiful and most inexpensive of antiques. They will undoubtedly become more valuable as the twentieth century marches further away from the age of the horse.

The idea of ornamenting harness with engraved brass plates is at least 3,000 years old. The Bible mentions 'ornaments on camels' necks'.

The original purpose was probably as a lucky charm to protect against harm, and one of the very earliest designs shows the sun's rays. The idea was that as the horse moved along the brightly polished metal reflected the sun's rays, and this was supposed to dazzle evil spirits and distract their attention. The Romans introduced this kind into Britain during the first century A.D. and some examples have been found on Roman sites at Caerleon in Wales. Brasses disappeared during the Dark Ages but received a new lease of life after the defeat of Napoleon, so that most of those available today are of the nineteenth century. Earlier ones are rare.

The variety of designs on the brasses is immense. A catalogue published in 1860 lists 330 different ones, but there were probably several thousands. Aristocrats had their heraldic designs engraved on their brasses, while other people used their trade or profession; this type is by far the most common. Horses working in dock areas usually had the symbol of St. Nicholas who was the patron saint of sailors. Canal horses had the same emblem. Breweries had a barrel, dairies a churn, millers a windmill, and so on. Brasses were frequently engraved with birds and other animals. Some can still be found bearing the prancing horse of Kent, a symbol which more than a thousand years before had decorated the banners of Saxon armies. A very interesting one shows an elephant and has the names 'Jumbo' and 'Alice'. These were two elephants which were popular at London Zoo in Victorian times. There was even a poem about them which went like this:

Jumbo said to Alice 'I love you.'
Alice said to Jumbo 'I don't believe you do.
If you really love me as you say you do
You would not go to Yankee Land and leave me in the Zoo.'

From 1837 to 1860 a popular series of brasses appeared made from a metal which very closely resembled gold. This was produced by a process invented by James Emerson using copper shot, finely calcined calamine and ground charcoal. Some brasses even showed nineteenth-century politician such as Gladstone and Disraeli. Others commemorated events like the Great Exhibition of 1851 in Hyde Park, the coronation of Queen Victoria and the end of the First World War.

From the 1850s gaily decorated dray and cart horses were common in the May Day processions. The great Shire horses, with their brasses polished and glittering, made a brave sight in the streets of England, and this spectacle continued well into the present century. Railway horses were always prominent in processions; and the brasses which they wore were engraved with the various types of locomotives.

16th Century *15th Century*

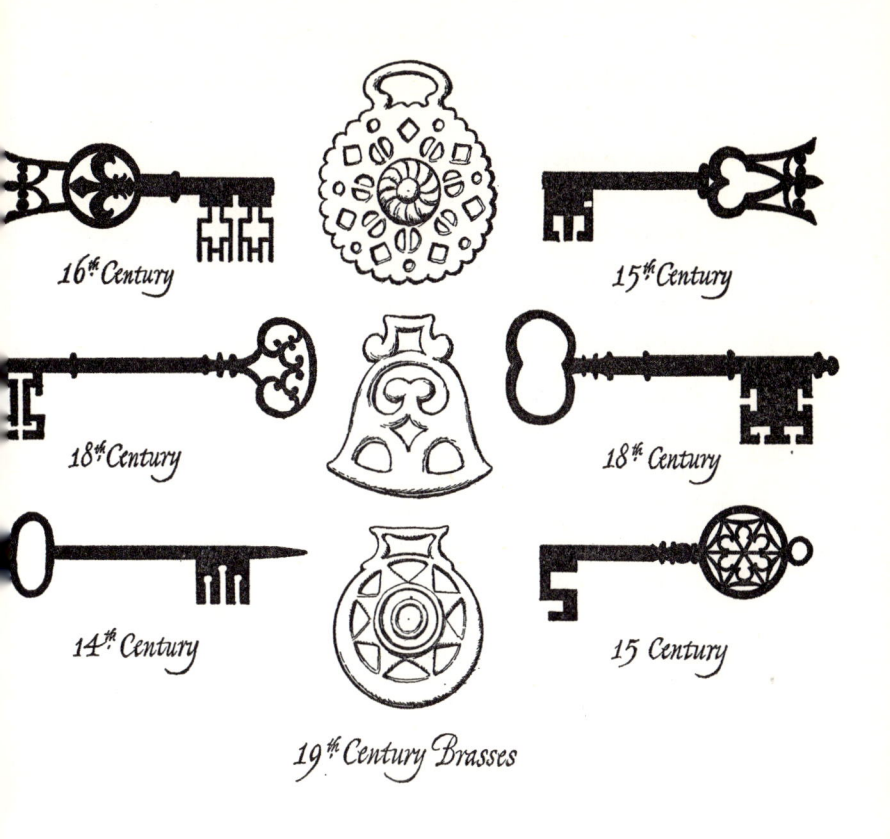

18th Century *18th Century*

14th Century *15 Century*

19th Century Brasses

A horse fully equipped with a complete set of brasses would have seven different kinds as follows:

Ear Brasses: One of these went behind each ear.
Flyers: These were fixed over the horse's head and swung loosely in a frame. Sometimes they had a red, white and blue brush or perhaps a bell attached.
Face Brasses: One or more of these hung over the horse's forehead.

[39]

Martingale Brasses: These were fastened on to the Martingale strap which came down from the collar and was fixed to the girth between the forelegs.

Hames: These were horn-shaped plates on each side of the collar.

Runner Brasses: Three of these went on each side of the runners on the horse's shoulders.

Noseband Plates: There were a varying number of these.

Thousands of brasses are made today as tourist souvenirs, but they are not sufficiently valuable for fakers to go to any great trouble over, and it is fairly easy to tell the modern from the genuine antique. Always look for signs of wear in places where the brass should have rubbed against the leather through years of use.

Horse brasses are easy to find and not expensive. It is possible to make quite a large collection without having any two the same.

FURTHER READING

Horse Brasses by George Hartfield (Abelard-Schuman)
Collecting Copper & Brass by Geoffrey Wills (Archer House)

9
Door Knockers and Porters

THE time is the Middle Ages. The place in front of a church. Panting, gasping, casting terrified glances behind him, a man in ragged clothes stumbles through the gates and collapses on to the porch of the church.

'Get him! Catch the scoundrel!' shout the armed men who have pursued the fugitive for hours and are nearly as exhausted as he is.

Fear gives the man renewed strength. He scrambles to his feet, grasps the iron ring which protrudes from the carved head of a lion fastened to the door and bangs it vigorously. The noise it makes is not very loud because the ring is hitting only the wood; there is no metal plate for it to sound upon.

The pursuers reach the porch – and stop suddenly. One man raises his sword but the officer in charge freezes him with a word of command.

'Let him be. He has claimed holy sanctuary.'

Slowly the man lowers his weapon and they all back away, scowling and furious. The great door swings open and a priest stands there.

'Father!' the fugitive exclaims. 'Let me in. I claim sanctuary.'

The priest says nothing but merely opens the door a little wider and the man stumbles inside. As some of the pursuers surge forward the priest raises his hand. 'This man has

A First Book of Antiques

claimed the shelter of the Church,' he says firmly. 'Let no man defy the Law of Sanctuary.' He closes the door firmly. The men swear, then at an order from the officer turn away.

That was a scene enacted many thousands of times during the Middle Ages when any man fleeing from the law could claim protection in the Church. Once inside he was safe for only the most evil and degenerate would ever dare to invade the holy house. It was even enough that his hand was on the iron ring held in the lion's mouth. To have hold of it was to be safe.

The doors of houses had a similar ring though without the lion's head. Later, in Elizabethan times, visitors announced themselves by rapping on the door with a wooden stave. It was the custom then for people to carry staves about with them as a means of protection in a lawless age before there were police forces; but sometimes the householder would leave a mallet hanging on a nail outside his door for the convenience of any visitors who might not be carrying their own staves.

The first true knockers developed naturally from the rings on the church doors in the late sixteenth century when blacksmiths began to make them in the shape of a mallet. They later provided a metal plate on to which the knocker could resound.

When knockers began to be mass produced they just consisted of an iron piece swinging from pivots attached to a thin plate nailed to the door. This often proved to be a great attraction for young hooligans who tried their strength at the sport of knocker-wrenching. Largely because of this the pivoted rapper went out of fashion in the latter part of the eighteenth century.

Sanctuary door knocker, Durham

The blacksmiths then developed more secure and elaborate knockers made of cast instead of wrought iron. Animal-head shapes with the knocker swinging freely from mouth or nostrils became fashionable. Some rappers were in the form of a fruiting vine or of a hand clutching a bar; and in the 1760s a vogue for classical designs brought the vase shape and the sphinx head. By 1839 the firm of Coalbrookdale (also known as Coalport) had produced castings which could be hand-chased and highly burnished.

A favourite collector's item today is the knocker which has a diamond-shaped mark showing that the design was registered between 1842 and 1883.

Alongside with the later development of knockers was that of the door porter, an ornamental door stop, usually made of brass or iron and dating from 1775 onwards.

Early examples were often shaped like a basket of flowers

A First Book of Antiques

or a lion's paw. Sometimes they were quite heavy and large. A crouching lion or a sphinx could be as high as 15 inches and weigh 3 or 4 pounds. In the middle of the nineteenth century there was a fashion for making porters in imitation of celebrated figures such as Napoleon, Wellington in his cocked hat, or Queen Victoria in her coronation robes. Punch and Judy were favourites.

There are certain rarer types, eagerly sought now by collectors, such as obelisks of Derbyshire marble, and domes of clear green glass with long-drawn air bubbles inside; most of these were made by the Bristol firm of Nailsea from 1828.

There are knockers and porters in a number of museums, in particular the Old Merchant's House in Great Yarmouth and the Victoria and Albert Museum. The largest and most extraordinary collection in the whole of Europe is to be found in Normandy in the town of Rouen – famous for its memories of Joan of Arc – where there are thousands of items from all over the Continent. For the would-be collector the best sources of knockers and porters are the sales held at old country houses.

FURTHER READING

The Coming Collecting Boom by John Mebane (A. S. Barnes).
Collecting Copper & Brass by Geoffrey Wills (Archer House).

10
Locks and Keys

LOCKS and keys have been with us almost ever since man invented doors and became suspicious of his fellow creatures. They are pictured in paintings on the walls of tombs in the Nile Valley, and the very earliest ones that we know of were Egyptian and were made of wood.

It was probably about 1000 B.C. that the daring Phoenician traders arrived on the coast of Cornwall to buy Cornish tin and river pearls from the British; and they brought with them a type of pin-lock made in hardwood. The Britons soon learned to copy these locks in the finest native oak, and actually continued doing so right up to the Victorian age. It was one of Britain's longest surviving crafts.

The Romans made keys and locks of metal from quite an early period, and their women often wore tiny keys as rings. Sometimes these were the keys to jewel boxes.

In Britain the first metal locks were manufactured in the reign of King Alfred (849–899) and the craft was well established by the twelfth century. During the Middle Ages, when doors often had very elaborate carvings on them, some were made in a cunning fashion so that sections of the sculptured work had to be moved aside in a certain order to cause a hidden bolt to retract. This idea might be described as the first combination lock.

But it was not until the sixteenth century that any real

attempt was made to produce keys and locks that were also works of art, with elaborate carving and decoration. The finest examples of all were made by French locksmiths in the sixteenth and seventeenth centuries. The beauty of their steel work and the quality of decoration has never been bettered. These are collectors' items worth searching for, though one has to be careful of imitations. There was a vogue for collecting French examples during the nineteenth century and many thousands of fakes were produced to meet the demand.

Brass-cased locks date from the late sixteenth century, and the improvements in the technique of brass-making resulted in some fine products in this period.

Some of the best British locks were made by a man whose name, extraordinarily enough, was Joseph *Key*! He held a royal appointment as a locksmith in the early eighteenth century and his name appears on many magnificent locks.

It is always easier to find keys than locks, for the simple reason that for every lock at least two keys were usually made. Collecting these two items is at present a far more popular custom in America than Britain. There they even collect keys of money-boxes, clocks, dog-collars and pianos! We usually follow America in these trends so the fashion will certainly spread here, and that means that the best time to collect locks and keys is now, before prices begin to rise.

FURTHER READING

The Coming Collecting Boom by John Mebane (A. S. Barnes).

II

Chinese Porcelain

PORCELAIN is a type of ceramic which is fired at a high temperature in the kiln and is made from a special kind of clay called kaolin. One difference between pottery and porcelain is that if you hold a piece of porcelain up to the light you will see that it is translucent. Also it is very much harder than pottery and cannot easily be marked with a knife.

The Chinese were the first people to invent hard paste porcelain as well as so many other things, from the magnetic compass to glass, silk and the printing-press.

When Britain was still a barbaric land of feuding Saxon kingdoms, struggling to emerge from the dark ages that followed the fall of Rome, the wealthy nobles and merchants of far-away China were handling beautiful vases decorated in the style of the Sung dynasty (960–1279).

It was Marco Polo, when he brought back the first of these vases that Europe had ever seen, who called the material 'porcelain'. The name comes from the Italian *'porcellana'*, a small sea shell which has a very lustrous surface not unlike porcelain.

Chinese porcelain is always described according to the dynasty in which it was made; and the Sung was followed by the famous Ming dynasty (1368–1644) when there was more elaborate decoration on vases and other objects than previously. Then came the lengthy Manchu dynasty (1644–1912) which included the rich colouring and ornamentation of the K'ang-hsi period.

In the early days of European enthusiasm for Chinese wares the French were among the most eager collectors and gave names to the colourings which have remained in use ever since. We refer to *famille rose, famille verte* and *famille noire* for red, green and black. There is also the very rare *famille jaune* meaning yellow. The colours refer to the main tint used on a particular piece and not to the general background colour. There is an exception with famille noire which usually has a black background relieved by colours such as green and white or perhaps vermilion. Pieces in famille rose or famille verte have some of the white porcelain left visible for effect and are usually decorated with pictures of flowers and the customary elongated Chinese figures in panels.

Of the three main dynasties it was the Sung which produced some of the most beautiful shapes and spectacular glazes. There are the opalescent blue and purple *Chün* and the *Chien* tea bowls. The plant and animal designs are both features of the Sung.

With the rise of the Ming dynasty the emperors gave much more money and patronage to the porcelain industry and this led to very rich and colourful decoration with thick glazing. Dragons, floral designs and landscapes with thin figures on terraces were used a great deal.

Finally the Ming dynasty produced some of the finest white porcelain with a brilliant sapphire blue decoration. There is also a whole range of famille verte tea-sets and eggshell-thin plates and bowls painted with flowers.

If you study carefully the designs on vases and plates you

will see the various subjects which the artists used for decoration over hundreds of years, many of them connected with the religions of Buddhism, Confucianism and Taoism and including numerous mythological figures and symbols.

There is the *yin yang*, a divided circle which symbolizes the natural duality of many things, such as male and female, black and white, hot and cold and so forth. The very ancient symbol of the swastika appears, and various cloud-and-thunder shapes.

Then there are the Four Supernatural Creatures:

1 The Dragon symbolizing the power of air and water.
2 The Tortoise for strength and long life.
3 The Kylin, a very mixed-up creature which has a dragon's head, a bushy tail and the hoofs of a deer. It symbolizes the power of Good.
4 The Phoenix, which was originally chosen as the emblem of an empress and the meaning of which nobody really knows.

Flowers have many symbolisms in Chinese mythology. There are the Twelve Flowers of the Month, the Lotus Lily for Purity and the Flowers of the Four Seasons. Then there are the Four Accomplishments: Music: a lyre case. Games: a chequer board. Painting: pair of scrolls. Literature: a pair of books.

Other symbols are the Eight Precious Objects: Money, jewel, lozenge, pair of books, painting, hanging jade musical stone, rhinoceros horn cup, artemisia leaf.

The marks on the best Chinese porcelain were very carefully inscribed by skilled calligraphers, but there has been so much faking that marks are not always reliable. The design

A First Book of Antiques

and colouring are better guides to the period and age, but to recognize these takes a lot of experience.

When Europeans began to settle in Chinese cities along the coast the porcelain which they bought and sent back home was, naturally, made originally for Chinese buyers; but by the seventeenth century the Chinese merchants had realized that there was much money to be made by the manufacture of special porcelain for export to the lands of the 'foreign devils'.

Contact with French Jesuit priests who settled in China about 1600 was responsible for plates and dishes with pictures of the crucifix and other Christian designs, often side by side with Buddhist symbols. The Chinese craftsmen considered that the Christian symbols were evidently of importance to the white man who would obviously welcome them on his table-ware, and a little propaganda for the Buddhist faith at the same time would be a good idea. The Chinese merchants were always willing to suit their wares to their customers. They exported vessels to Japan painted with pictures of the Japanese tea ceremony, and plates to Islamic countries decorated with verses from the Koran. In the eighteenth century when wealthy Europeans and Americans wanted their family crests on vases, plates and dishes the Chinese provided them.

When they painted scenes of a supposedly typical English or Italian garden you will often find, on looking carefully, a lotus peeping from among the European flowers. The Chinese soon found out about other scenes which the white people apparently liked to have painted, and punch-bowls began to appear with pictures of fox-hunting, or copies of famous European paintings. Hogarth was one whose works were often copied.

Chinese Porcelain

Much table-ware and many domestic ornaments were produced by the Chinese in what they believed to be the Western taste. There were flowerpots, salt and pepper containers, snuff-boxes, tankards and even imitations of Toby Jugs. One thing which the Orientals were never able to get quite right, however, was the European face. This defeated them, and on many items you will see pictures of peasants or aristocratic court figures with distinctly Oriental faces.

From the seventeenth century onwards the Chinese produced vast quantities of porcelain for export and they called this 'Yang Ch'I' which means foreign vessels. A letter from the French East India Company to a Canton merchant read 'Send us no more dragons but let us have flowers instead.'

The best of the Chinese porcelain, such as the famous Ming vases, and those of the Sung dynasty, is usually to be found only in museums or private collections, but the later porcelains, especially of the export type, can still be found for sale – and not always at high prices.

FURTHER READING

Early Chinese Pottery & Porcelain by Basil Gray (Faber & Faber).

Later Chinese Porcelain by Soame Jenyns (Faber & Faber).

12
Meissen Porcelain

'A ROGUE and a charlatan' is not the description which one would expect of a man who made one of mankind's most important discoveries; but it is a true description of Johann Böttger, the first person who found out how to make porcelain in Europe.

When Marco Polo brought the first porcelain vases back to Europe in 1295 after his historic journey to China (see Chapter 11) the material was a great wonder to Europeans. Everyone was amazed at its hardness and beautiful glossy surface. The famous cobalt blue Ming vases were especially admired and it soon became the ambition of kings and aristocrats to possess these marvellous ornaments.

After Polo's adventure some porcelain began to come along the caravan trails that wound through the high wilderness of Central Asia. Later still, when the great navigators such as Vasco da Gama and Henry the Navigator had opened up the eastern sea routes to the 'fabulous land of Cathay', as China was known, the ships of the East India companies began to bring back cargoes of porcelain. This came to be called 'china' during the seventeenth century and onwards.

It was this greater availability which really aroused the collecting passion in Europe and caused porcelain to become almost a form of currency.

One man, Augustus the Strong, King of Poland and Elec-

Meissen Porcelain

tor of Saxony, became fanatically determined to own the greatest collection of porcelain on the Continent. He spent so much of his country's money on this that it is even said that he once gave the King of Prussia a regiment of soldiers in exchange for forty-eight vases!

The dramatic story of how Europe found out how to make porcelain for itself began in 1704 when the young Johann Böttger arrived in the kingdom of Augustus after fleeing from Prussia where he had got into trouble through cheating merchants who had financed his pretended experiments to make gold. Alchemists all over Europe were seeking the 'philosopher's stone' with which they hoped to transmute base metals into gold.

Augustus's eyes gleamed when he heard about Johann. He had him arrested, imprisoned him in a castle near the town of Dresden, and commanded, 'Now make me gold so that I may buy more porcelain.' Poor Johann had no more idea how to make gold than anyone else; and for several years he laboured without result in the workshop that Augustus set up for him in the castle.

Then, just as the patience of his captor was wearing thin, Johann hit upon a brilliant idea. Since he could not make gold, and what the King really wanted was porcelain, why not make porcelain itself?

All over Europe people were making experiments to discover the great Chinese secret and it seemed unlikely that Johann would succeed; but he was fantastically lucky. He heard of a rare type of white clay – kaolin – which was mined near by and used for making the white powder which gentlemen put on their wigs. Experimenting with this Johann at last succeeded in making something very like the real

Chinese porcelain. It was not yet quite perfect but he had triumphed where so many had failed. The monopoly of China was broken.

Later placed over the entrance to Johann's laboratory was the inscription 'God, our creator, has made of a gold-maker a potter.'

Augustus established a factory at Meissen, which is a suburb of Dresden, and made Johann its director in 1710. Soon the factory produced the most beautiful vases and colourfully-painted figures, and quickly obtained a dominating influence throughout Europe which lasted for many years until other countries set up their own factories.

Items made at the Meissen factory in the eighteenth century are now very expensive and highly prized by collectors, especially the groups of figures, the ladies in flowing crinolines, shepherdesses and other peasant figures in which Meissen specialized.

J. J. Kändler who became chief modeller in 1733 was a creative genius who first recognized the artistic possibilities of the material. Breaking away from the Chinese influence which dominated European pottery for so long he designed superb Italian comedy figures, and birds that were studied from nature. His farm-and-garden themes, colourful and spectacular, became fashionable set-pieces for use as dining table ornaments.

The mark on the bottom of Meissen ware shows variations of the crossed swords which came from the royal coat of arms of Augustus. Sometimes other firms have faked Meissen products. Limbach, a German factory, made imitations of Meissen in the late eighteenth century and used as their mark a double 'L' in such a manner that many

Staffordshire, 1830

Chinese, 10th Cent. A.D.

Meissen, 1744

collectors were and still are deceived into believing it to be the crossed swords of Meissen.

The most highly prized of genuine Meissen items today are those bearing, not the crossed swords, but either a mark like a snake coiled round a pole or the letters 'KPM'. These were the very earliest marks used during Johann Böttger's directorship from 1710 until his death in 1719. It was in 1724 that the crossed swords mark was adopted and has been used ever since.

Many other factories were established in Dresden and their products are referred to as Dresden porcelain, but Meissen ware comes only from the original factory which is still producing beautiful objects.

FURTHER READING

Dresden China by W. B. Honey (A. & C. Black)
The Complete Encyclopaedia of Antiques (The Connoisseur).
(See pages 924–6)

13
Spode Porcelain

SPODE was especially famous for having invented three distinct methods of producing a soft-paste substitute for the Continental hard-paste porcelain. The original porcelain invented by Johann Böttger at Meissen was a hard paste, which means that it had to be fired twice in the kiln. Soft paste needs firing only once.

There were three Josiah Spodes, father, son and grandson, and the original Josiah founded his factory in 1770. The early products were ordinary earthenware pottery but in the 1790s Spode began producing porcelain, and when the second Josiah took over from his father in 1797 he transformed the whole scene of English porcelain manufacture.

In 1794 the Government had imposed an import duty of 30 per cent on all Continental porcelains except those from Holland. This made it very expensive to import into Britain and caused British firms to search for a cheaper substitute for the hard pastes of Meissen and other factories.

Josiah Spode II led this search and was the first to succeed. He produced bone china made from animal bones reduced to a fine powder by heat. The result was a fine milky-white porcelain, thin, with a clear ring when tapped. It also had the advantage that it did not discolour with time as did some hard pastes. The designs of Spode's bone china were mostly based on those of China's export porcelain, for British potters at that time were still fascinated by Chinese designs.

In 1805 Josiah II invented stone china which was not quite so fine and glossy, and in 1815 came his third discovery: feldspar china which proved to be the whitest porcelain ever produced in Britain.

Josiah II died in 1827 and was followed by his son who unfortunately was able to carry on the line for only two years, since he died in 1829.

The factory was bought by a William Taylor Copeland in 1833 and thereafter its products were often known as Spode-Copeland, though the mark always uses the full name of Spode only; this has been so since 1790. Beware, however, of Spode pieces marked 'Bone China'; this mark has only been put on since 1900 and such pieces are too recent to be classed as antique.

Spode made, as well as dinner services and tea-sets, large model animals, plaques and fire-place slabs. The factory also produced some of the unglazed Parian ware which looks like marble.

FURTHER READING

British Pottery & Porcelain 1780–1850 by G. A. Godden (Arthur Barker)

14
Worcester Porcelain

WORCESTER porcelain differs from other varieties in that it contains Cornish soap-stone. It has a slightly greenish tinge when light shines through it, and is known as a soft paste because it is fired at a lower temperature than Meissen and other Continental hard pastes.

The factory was founded by a Dr Wall in 1751, and in 1752 the *Gentleman's Magazine* announced that, 'There will be a sale of china made at the new factory. The sale will begin at the music meeting on September 20.'

That sale was the start of one of the most famous names in British porcelain. During the 'First Period', as it is called, which lasted until 1783, Worcester concentrated upon making items which were mainly of practical use, such as teapots, jugs, tankards and so on.

Most of that early work was unmarked and is highly decorative with an underglaze blue relieved by white panels on which are painted scenes, very often copied from the Chinese, showing figures against a landscape, or flowers and exotic birds. From the 1750s a mark began to appear. Sometimes this was 'W' sometimes a square Chinese mark which deceived some people. Often Worcester committed the sin of using the Meissen crossed swords! This was not the only compliment which Worcester paid to the great factory in Dresden during the Dr Wall period: there was also a lot of deliberate copying of the familiar Meissen floral designs. From about 1760 a crescent mark appeared, though it should be noted that this was also used by Caughley, Lowestoft and Bow.

Worcester of the First Period can be divided into three classes. The first, transfer printing, in which the artists pioneered the delicate process of transferring copper-plate engravings on to the surface of the material over the glaze. A famous artist, Robert Hancock, was among those who worked on this process and some of the early wares are marked with his name.

The second class, which began to appear in the late 1760s, was the coloured ware. This had rich and striking pinks, blues, yellows and – more rarely – brick red. There was also a pea-green borrowed from Sèvres. Rarest of all is the claret. Artists came from Chelsea to work on the colour process and used many foreign sources for their inspiration: Japanese, Chinese, Meissen, Sèvres are all copied or used as a basis for variations.

The third class of the Dr Wall era was the blue and white. Worcester, like the Chinese centuries before, found out that cobalt was the easiest of all colours when it came to controlling the process in the kiln, and in their blue-and-white wares they made a wide range of objects including tureens, cabbage-leaf jugs, pierced baskets, cups and saucers, sauceboats, salad bowls and many other items of table-ware. Typical pictures are of ducks swimming under bridges, birds in rushes, dragons and the inevitable long thin Oriental ladies with parasols known as Long Elizas, a name which comes from the Dutch term *lange lijsen* meaning literally 'long figure'.

Worcester Porcelain

In 1788 King George III and Queen Charlotte visited Worcester and from then on the title Royal was added to the name, and the crescent mark which was then in use was given a crown.

Earlier, in 1783, the factory had been bought by a Thomas Flight, thus ending the period of Dr Wall, and in later years a number of different marks appear. There are variations of the name Flight, which was later added to by that of Martin Barr who joined the company. Sometimes the initials of both are used in different combinations.

The use of Cornish soap-stone gave to Worcester one special quality – that of withstanding heat better than any other porcelain. This was especially valuable with teapots. When other porcelains went brown and cracked with the years of hot brewings Worcester stayed the same.

Once you have seen some Worcester, the blue-and-white in particular is easy to recognize, even though very similar wares were made by certain other factories – notably Caughley of Shropshire.

FURTHER READING

British Pottery and Porcelain 1780–1850 by G. A. Godden (Arthur Barker).
Worcester Porcelain by S. Fisher (Ward Lock).

15
Staffordshire Pottery Figures

' My casts are formed to get my bread,
And humble shelter for my head.'

THAT was the plaintive cry of the 'image men' who roamed the countryside during the latter part of the eighteenth century and most of the nineteenth. They were selling Staffordshire pottery figures which were being turned out in tens of thousands.

So popular were they and so easy to sell that in some of the bigger potteries child labour was employed in primitive conditions. A report on this 'slave labour' quoted the statement by nine-year-old William Cotton who was questioned by members of the committee making the report.

'How many of these earthenware figures do you make in an hour, William?' they asked him.

'Forty-two,' he replied.

'And how many hours in a week do you work?'

'I work seventy-two.'

'And how much are you paid?'

'I am paid 2s every week.'

It was a long time before these evils were righted, and today the figures which those half-starved children helped to make are eagerly sought by antique collectors. They seem to be especially popular with the Dutch and Italians, to whom thousands of them are now going, often at high prices. To

Bristol c.1760 Staffordshire c.1675 Longton Hall c.1755

the ordinary collector, and especially to the beginner, Staffordshire earthenware figures represent one of the easiest and most inexpensive objects to acquire.

Staffordshire ware mostly comes from the area known as 'The Potteries', comprising the small towns of Burslem, Fenton, Hanley, Shelton, Longport and Stoke-on-Trent.

The nineteenth-century novelist Arnold Bennett referred to the region as the 'Black Country', also as 'The Smoke'; and it is easy to understand these names when one drives along certain roads even today and sees the great cloud drifting from the chimneys of the kilns.

Staffordshire is rich in suitable clays, and pottery was a peasant art there more than 300 years ago. In the seventeenth

A First Book of Antiques

and eighteenth centuries at the end of a thousand country lanes were the bottle-shaped kilns belonging to small farmers. Often the cow shed would stand side by side with the 'throwing shed' in which pots and vases were 'thrown' on the potter's wheel.

For a long time it was a fairly crude type that these peasants made; but then in the late seventeenth century two Dutch potters settled in the county. They were the brothers Elers, who showed them how to improve their ware and give it a fine glaze by throwing salt into the kiln. By the early years of the nineteenth century this salt-glaze pottery was becoming well known, especially in the form of the numerous figures which found a ready demand.

Among the earliest kind were the so-called pew groups; these were flat-backed models of people either singly or in groups, always in front of a high-backed pew or at least what seemed like a pew, though there is some doubt about whether it was really intended to be that. The figures were often shown playing flutes or holding hands; ladies had dogs on their laps, and it does not seem likely that they actually sat in church in such a carefree fashion.

There were also lovers under spreading trees and the bell women whose large skirts stood out like bells. There were many other groups, too, such as two ladies pouring out tea for a visiting vicar while a dog leaps up to lick him; or rustic scenes of men sitting drinking outside public houses.

Dogs were very popular as subjects and almost every breed ever known has been modelled in Staffordshire ware, usually in pairs so that they could be placed at opposite ends of the mantelpiece. Greyhounds were firm favourites and were shown standing or lying down. Since greyhounds were not

Staffordshire Pottery Figures

used for racing in those days but only for the alleged 'sport' of coursing they were often modelled holding a hare in the mouth. Another breed which frequently appears is the one known as the 'comforter' because it was a very pampered animal spending most of its time being nursed by wealthy old ladies. These dogs were usually painted white with coloured ears, several spots on the body, a pink nose, and eyes that are almost human. A gilded chain lay round the neck. There were also droopy poodles carrying baskets in their mouths, and pastoral groups of sheep.

Among the famous names of Staffordshire ware are those of Ralph and Aaron Wood. Their pottery was thinner than most, though it thickened as the eighteenth century advanced. It usually has a hollow base with an unglazed interior. Their humans and animals frequently stand on rocks and some of the people are splendid creations showing details usually found only in porcelain.

The Woods made anatomically correct figures of Greek gods and goddesses, and whole orchestras of musicians in wonderful colour harmonies made by a clever combination of metallic oxides. To obtain blue they used cobalt (as the Chinese had done on porcelain centuries before them), for purple, manganese, copper for green and iron for yellow.

The Woods also specialized in teapots, some of which tend to be comical. One popular design is shaped like an elephant with a rider which is the lid. A huge python is coiling itself up one of the elephant's hind legs and rearing itself to strike at the rider while serving also as the handle.

There was Felix Pratt who made figures, in very loud colours, called 'Prattware'. The early examples are often crude and ugly but later their standard became much higher.

A First Book of Antiques

John Walton of Burslem was famous for his white figures of shepherdesses, gardeners, fisherwomen and biblical characters. These were often on fairly high bases which had stunted trees rising at the back.

One of the most famous of Staffordshire items is the Toby Jug with the front in the shape of a man's face. The original design was based on the story of a Yorkshireman with the unlikely name of Toby Fillpot who is said to have drunk 2,000 gallons of beer without eating anything from the first gallon to the last, though it is not known how long this took him. There is a great variety of Toby Jugs and some collectors have hundreds – all different.

The Victorians were fond of depicting criminals, and Oliver and Martha Sherratt were two Staffordshire potters who specialized in the more gruesome ones. They made models of notorious murderers, one of the most well-known examples being a little cottage which was really supposed to be the barn of the Victorian melodrama *Maria Marten and the Murder in the Red Barn*. The cottage, or barn, has the doomed Maria standing on one side of it and her murderer, William Corder, wicked son of the squire, on the other. The Fitzwilliam Museum in Cambridge and Brighton Museum have excellent examples of the red barn and other 'murder' pieces.

The Sherratts also made groups showing married couples quarrelling, figures of royalty and other famous people including the highwayman Dick Turpin, and Grace Darling, the daughter of a lighthouse keeper who rowed a small boat in a storm to rescue shipwrecked sailors. Other Sherratt models show the eighteenth-century actor James Quinn as Falstaff and the actor-manager David Garrick as Richard III.

Staffordshire Pottery Figures

There are also sporting figures such as cricketers, boxers and jockeys, and characters from opera.

John Astbury was another of the pioneers of Staffordshire, specializing in Adam and Eve figures. His pottery is recognizable by crude lines and the lack of distinctive features.

One characteristic of nineteenth-century Staffordshire ware and of some eighteenth century is that an aging process takes place which causes what dealers call 'crazing'. This is a pattern of irregular shapes which spreads all over the piece. It is accepted as a sign of a genuine antique because modern Staffordshire ware still being produced is not old enough for this effect to have developed. The absence of crazing, however, does not mean that a piece is not old. The type of material used by the Woods and by John Walton did not usually craze at all.

One has to beware of faking. Some people found out that by immersing a figure in horse manure the natural ammonia speeded up the aging process and caused the crazing to appear within a matter of days so that customers were often deceived into thinking that it was a real antique. Today the same effect is produced by a chemical method in the factory, and there is nothing illegal about it providing the object is not actually advertised as an antique; but there are always dishonest dealers who forget to mention that such an item is modern.

It is useful to know that the artificial crazing has smaller and more uniform squares than the natural, and the modern pieces usually have much brighter paint than the old ones.

FURTHER READING
Staffordshire Portrait Figures of the Victorian Age by Thomas Bolston (Faber & Faber).
Staffordshire Pottery Figures by John Bedford (Cassell).

16

Wedgwood Pottery
The Four Great Discoveries
of Josiah Wedgwood

ONE of the most famous types of British pottery is the blue-and-white Wedgwood ware to be seen in the windows of most shops which sell both antique and modern ceramics; but this blue-and-white, known as 'Jasper Ware', is only one of the several kinds of beautiful pottery created by Josiah Wedgwood.

The romance of the Wedgwood story began when Josiah was born in 1730, in Burslem, Stoke-on-Trent. He could hardly have escaped his destiny since he was the third generation of a family of potters. Josiah's education began at the age of six when he had to walk seven miles a day to school at Newcastle-under-Lyne. School, however, did not last long. When he was nine his father died and Josiah was apprenticed to his elder brother at the Churchyard Pottery to learn what was then called the 'Art, Mistery, Occupation or Imployment of Throwing and Handleing.'

At the end of his apprenticeship he went into partnership with John Harrison, then in 1759 he founded the firm of Wedgwood and shortly afterwards produced the first of several famous inventions. This was a clear green glaze which he used to decorate leaf and vegetable shapes.

1. The drawing-room designed and furnished by Robert Adam at Osterley Park House, Middlesex. *(By courtesy of the Victoria and Albert Museum)*

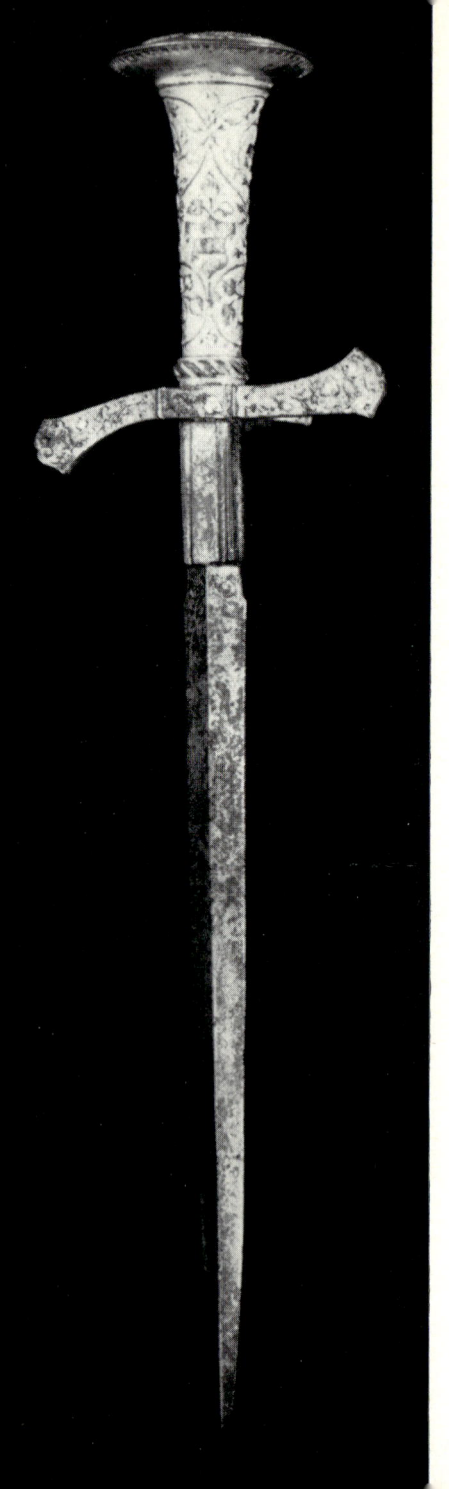

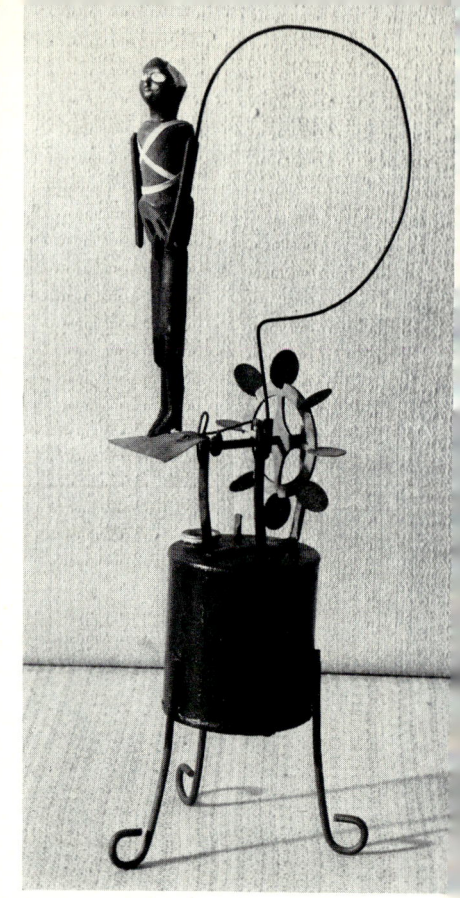

2. *Above:* A Victorian dancing soldier worked by jets of steam produced in the drum. These spin the large wheel causing both the platform and the wire suspending the soldier to jerk. *(The London Museum)*

3. *Left:* 16th-century German dagger made of iron and inlaid with gilt. *(By courtesy of the Victoria and Albert Museum)*

Wedgwood Pottery

In 1762 his second invention appeared on the market and examples of this are eagerly sought by collectors today. He described it as: 'A species of earthenware for the table, quite new in appearance, covered with a rich and brilliant glaze, bearing sudden alterations of heat and cold, manufactured with ease and expedition, and consequently cheap.'

Wedgwood knew the value of publicity, especially the kind that can be obtained by association with royalty, and in 1765 he presented a cream ware breakfast set to Queen Charlotte (consort of George III). It was painted in quiet natural colours with raised sprigs of flowers, and much of the cream ware produced afterwards followed similar designs. The Queen was enraptured by this new and beautiful table-ware and commanded that it be known as Queen's Ware.

In previous times the rich used only silver or porcelain on their tables, but Josiah, with his Queen's Ware, had put fine pottery within reach of all but the poorest, and its success was world-wide. In 1767 he wrote, 'The demand for this cream colour, alias Queen's Ware, still increases. It is amazing how rapidly the use of it has spread almost over the whole globe.'

In 1774 he undertook for Catherine of Russia the largest and most famous commission of his career: the creation of a dinner and dessert service of 952 pieces decorated with 1244 freehand paintings. Part of this service has survived the troubles of history and can be viewed today in the Hermitage Museum in Leningrad.

In 1764 he had married his cousin Sarah, a shrewd and charming personality of whom he wrote, 'I speak from experience in female taste, without which I should have made but a poor figure among my pots, not one of which of any consequence is finished without the approbation of my Sally.'

On June 13, 1769, he formally opened his brand-new pottery situated between Hanley and Newcastle-under-Lyne. He called it 'Etruria', and it held a dominant position in British pottery from then until 1940 when a modern factory was opened at Barlaston. It was at Etruria that he developed the third of his inventions – Egyptian Black Basalt – and no modern antique dealer's window can be said to be complete without some example of it.

Not everyone likes black objects, and some people dislike this material; but there is no doubt that it has its attractions, especially when highly polished and contrasted with more colourful pottery. Josiah described his discovery in rather high-flown terms as, 'A black biscuit of nearly the same properties as the natural stone, striking fire from steel, receiving a high polish, serving as a touchstone for metal and resisting all acids and bearing without injury a strong fire.' When tea services were made of Egyptian Black they showed to advantage the white hands of the hostess. In 1771 Josiah wrote to his partner, Thomas Bentley, 'I hope that white hands continue in fashion and then we may continue to make black teapots.'

All these discoveries, however – his green glaze, Queen's Ware, Egyptian Black – were but the preludes to the most successful of all Josiah Wedgwood's inventions: the renowned Jasper Ware. It was at Etruria in 1774 that, after more than 10,000 carefully recorded experiments, this supreme triumph of the potter's art was finally perfected.

Public taste in the eighteenth century was strongly influenced by the archaeological discoveries made at Pompeii and

Wedgwood Pottery

Herculaneum, and there was a great admiration for Greek and Roman art and a consequent search for a means of copying it. In particular a method was needed by which vases and other ornaments of antiquity could be reproduced. It was this search to which Josiah devoted his efforts immediately after moving into Etruria.

He sought far and wide for suitable raw material which other experimenters might have missed. He even sent a Mr John Griffiths to the American colonies charged with the mission of bringing back samples of a fine clay said to be used by the Cherokee Indians; and today there is a marker at Franklin, North Carolina, near the quarry from which the clay was obtained.

Success came at last and the Jasper body, variously coloured, was used in the manufacture of objects of every kind as well as tea and coffee services. There are flowerpots, paintboxes, snuff-boxes, bowls and even opera-glasses. Small cameos were set into items of furniture and into steel to make exquisite jewellery.

Models used for the figures on classical vases produced in Jasper during the early years came from various sources, the most famous of all the brilliant designers being John Flaxman, R.A. Among his creations is the well-known 'Dancing Hours' vase. At one period Josiah sent him to Rome where he founded a school of modellers and the designs and details were sent back to Etruria.

One of Wedgwood's greatest triumphs was the copying in Jasper of the famous Portland Vase. This unique object is one of the oldest vases ever discovered. Made of dark cobalt blue glass it was probably made in Alexandria in the first century A.D., and after being in the possession of the

Berberini family of Italy it came to Britain in the eighteenth century. The Duchess of Portland, of whom the writer Horace Walpole said, 'She is a simple woman, perfectly sober and intoxicated only by empty vases' kept a private museum of 'artificial curiosities' and bought the vase in 1784 for 1,800 guineas. Josiah obtained the loan of the precious object for a year so that he could study it and make a copy in Jasper. Later, in 1810, the vase was placed in the British Museum.

Tragedy struck it in 1845 when a young madman entered the Museum and brought a hammer crashing down on to the glass case which contained it. There were more than 200 fragments but the Museum craftsmen, using one of the Wedgwood copies as a guide, pieced it together and the vase can still be seen.

The best period for Jasper Ware was 1776 to 1806. The pieces produced in those years have a fine grain and a satiny feeling. The reliefs are carefully polished and finished, and are free from the dry chalkiness which became common in later periods.

The marks on the bottom of Wedgwood from 1769 to 1780 were either 'Wedgwood & Bentley' or simply 'W & B'. From 1780 to 1860 it was 'Josiah Wedgwood', and from 1860 it was 'Wedgwood' together with certain letter symbols which indicate the year of manufacture. Sometimes collectors can be deceived by the mark 'Wedgwood & Co.' This has nothing to do with any item produced at Etruria but belongs to pottery made by Ralph Wedgwood, a cousin of Josiah who owned a factory near Pontefract. There was also a J. Smith of Stockton who in 1848 made a quantity of items under the mark of Wedgewood with an 'e'.

Wedgewood Pottery

Today antique Wedgwood is amongst the most beautiful of all British pottery.

FURTHER READING

Wedgwood Ware by W. B. Honey (Faber & Faber)
Decorative Wedgwood by Alison Kelly (Country Life).
Antiques by Hampden Gordon (John Murray Paperback).

17
British Silver

SINCE very early times silver has been the second most precious metal after gold, and it has been used for centuries to make domestic and church ornaments, table-wares, swords, jewellery and a thousand other items; but of all the world's silver objects it is those made in Britain which are of the highest quality.

British silver has a content of ·925, which means that it contains ·925 parts of silver to 1,000 parts of metal, the remainder being usually copper. It is not possible to make things entirely of silver because the pure metal is very soft and would bend easily. It has to be mixed with copper to strengthen it. Continental and Oriental silver all contain a much higher proportion of copper or other supporting metal and are very hard by comparison.

British silver (and gold) is easily recognizable by the four types of marks which you find on every piece and which tell you a great deal about the history and origin of each item.

Since the year 1300 it has been law that the fineness of silver should be the same as that for coin, and that every piece must be weighed and its silver content 'assayed' at a Government Assay Office which then marks it with a symbol indicating that it contains ·925 of silver, and is therefore 'Sterling' silver. From 1300 the assay mark was a leopard's head but in 1544 this was changed to a lion *passant* (with one paw raised) and has remained so ever since.

The other marks which are found on every piece of silver are: the town mark which shows where the piece was assayed, the maker's mark and the date letter.

Several towns as well as London have their own assay offices and below is a list of the dates of these offices.

Birmingham	1773 (still in use today)
Glasgow	1819 (still in use today)
Chester	1701–1962
Newcastle	1721–1883
Dublin	1720 (still in use today)
Sheffield	1773 (still in use today)
Edinburgh	1681 (still in use today)
York	1559–1886
Exeter	1701–1883

Since 1478 the original leopard's head has been used for London's own town mark. Other towns have their own mark: Chester has a shield and sword, and Glasgow has a rather complicated one showing a tree, bell and a bird with a fish in its mouth.

The maker's mark usually consists of the initials of the silversmith, though in the Victorian period this was not always so. Sometimes the initials are those of a firm which commissioned the item for a customer.

The date letter shows the year in which the piece was hallmarked by an assay office. Ever since 1478 this has consisted of a letter of the alphabet from 'A' to 'U' but missing out 'J' which might be confused with 'I'. This means that there are twenty letters in all, one for each year and after twenty years they start at 'A' again. How do you know the year for which a letter stands? You do not unless you have one of the handbooks of marks which you can buy quite cheaply. Every time a new cycle of letters begins there is an alteration in the type of the letter and in the shape of the shield in which it is stamped. The handbooks explain all this.

Although the lion passant tells you that a piece is genuine Sterling silver there was one short period when this most familiar of all marks actually vanished. In 1697 the Government became alarmed at the practice of silversmiths of melting down coins and to stop this they introduced a higher standard of silver known as Britannia Standard. The figure of Britannia was then used by the offices until 1718 when it was replaced by the lion passant.

Silverware has often been faked. One well-known trick is to take a piece that is old and has become broken, remove the little patch containing the hallmark and fix it into a new piece. This can be detected if you breathe on the hallmark as the patch becomes visible. When you do buy a piece of antique silver the hallmark should never be polished. This gives it a new appearance and makes people think it is a fake.

The older silver items have often been repaired, sometimes very skilfully, but if the breath test is used any join will show up.

Another thing to look out for when buying a set of items, such as a tea or coffee set, is to see that all the marks are the same. Sometimes people buy one piece at a time to make up a set and then sell it; but in such cases the marks are different. This is not a fraud but it reduces the value of the set.

The variety of items that can be collected in old silver is infinite. It ranges from tea, coffee and dinner sets to trays,

Coffee pot 1773

Sauceboat 1754

Sugar caster 1672

Porringer 1683

Snuffers 1688

caddy spoons, epergnes, candlesticks, snuff-boxes, jewel boxes and almost every imaginable type of ornament.

A useful item to start collecting is a set of Apostle Spoons. These contain thirteen of which twelve are designed with the handle in the shape of an Apostle with his emblem. The thirteenth is a figure of Christ and is called the 'Master Spoon'. The Victoria and Albert Museum has the biggest collection of spoons in the world including Seal-Top Spoons, Puritan Spoons and many others.

We are fortunate that all items of silver are so clearly marked so that with a book of marks we can tell at a glance when a piece was made, the name of the firm that made it and where the metal was assayed. Marks can, however, be

A First Book of Antiques

faked. In fact, the experts usually look at the mark last of all when buying silver. Long experience has taught them to recognize its period by the feel, appearance and design of the piece.

In the Restoration period from 1660 the drinking of tea and coffee became popular and this created a new era in English domestic silver with the manufacture of elegant teapots and coffee-pots; a change from the previous age of the Puritan régime when extravagance in design was frowned upon. Then there was the Queen Anne period (1702–14) in which silver design was greatly influenced by Huguenot silversmiths who came to Britain from Northern France and preferred simplicity of outline. Later came the neo-classical movement which was inspired by the work of Robert Adam (1728–92) and roused great enthusiasm for the gracefulness of Greek classical shapes.

The expert knows these and other periods and influences and can usually assess the age and quality of a piece from this knowledge; but when we are only beginning we need constantly to refer to our book of marks – not forgetting a small magnifying glass without which most of the older marks are difficult or impossible to see.

Something else which the expert recognizes is the work of the famous designers. The eighteenth century was the great age of the well-known silversmiths whose initials appear on their work.

A famous designer was Hester Bateman. Her mark, 'HB', appears from 1774. When an expert sees an item with a particularly brightly cut engraving which catches the light and sparkles, he knows that it was probably by Hester Bateman, especially if it is a piece of table ware with a beaded border.

British Silver

Paul de Lamerie (mark 'LA' with a crown above the letters) is another name for which to look out. He specialized in figure engraving from 1712. One of the most colourful personalities was Nicholas Sprimont, an eccentric character who came from Liège, in Belgium, and was one of the Huguenots who settled in Britain. Sprimont often drove through London in a gilded chariot drawn by two horses; and his name is preserved in Chelsea in Sprimont Place. He later turned his attention from silver to porcelain and was one of the founders of the Chelsea porcelain factory.

Scottish silver is not so very different from English except that it was not made until the late seventeenth century. The ornamentation tends to be simpler than the English and such items as thistle cups are engraved with the Scottish thistle; but apart from these characteristics it has few obvious Scottish signs about it. The marks for this silver can be found in the Scottish section of the book *English Goldsmiths and Their Marks* by Sir Charles Jackson.

Irish silver suffered a great decline during the seventeenth century when Cromwell laid much of the country waste. The guild to which Irish silversmiths belonged virtually ceased to exist and vast amounts of plate were melted down. After 1700 there was a rapid recovery, and the best period for Irish silver is reckoned to be from 1720 to 1820. Dublin silver especially is highly prized by collectors with its mark of a crowned harp, the figure of Hibernia being added in 1730.

When searching for silver remember that it tarnishes quickly with the passing years, and can look very uninteresting in a dark corner of a shop, so do not be put off by appearances. Silver is expensive as a metal, apart from being an antique. When in doubt consult an expert before buying.

FURTHER READING

Collecting English Silver by Mona Curran (Arco Publications)
English Domestic Silver by Charles Oman (Adam & Charles Black)
The Lure of Antiques by Hampden Gordon (John Murray Paperback)

18
Old Sheffield Plate

ANGRY silversmiths of Sheffield in the late eighteenth century denounced Sheffield Plate as a fraud upon the public; and well they might resent it, for the discovery that objects could look like solid silver and yet contain only a fraction of the usual amount came as a great blow to them.

The method first became known one day in the 1740s when Thomas Bolsover, a Sheffield cutler, called on his friend George Fairbottom.

'What brings you here, Thomas?' said George. 'You are not in trouble, I hope?'

'Not trouble, Thomas; I bring good news,' he paused, and looked round. 'There is no one listening, I trust?'

George was surprised. 'In my house, of course not.'

'No one must know my secret until I am ready. George, I have discovered how to make articles of silver and use only a quarter – or even less – of the silver itself. Yet I do swear to you that the result will look the same, and 'twill not be a fraud, either.'

'If this be true then it is a great and startling thing that you have done.'

'It is true, upon my oath it is. I was in my workshop but a month ago repairing a knife when I accidentally touched a piece of copper with the heated silver and the two did fuse solidly together. It gave me an idea and I experimented. I found that by heating a plate of copper and a thin sheet of silver the two would fasten together and could then be rolled and beaten, aye, just as if they were one.'

George Fairbottom began to see what he meant. 'And it will look just like the solid silver?'

'Aye, that it will – and for much less of a price. I need but some money to perfect my experiments. George, my friend, if you will loan me £170 it will be sufficient and you shall soon be repaid.'

George Fairbottom readily agreed and with this money Bolsover started a business making silver-plated buttons; but, although he prospered, he did not have the vision and the enterprise to build a large business.

To him belongs the honour of discovering Sheffield Plate but it was another man, Matthew Boulton who, in partnership with James Watt – the discoverer of steam power – went into the silver-plating business on such a scale that the silversmiths became alarmed. Boulton and his partner used to meet at a public house in Sheffield called *The Crown and Anchor*, and it was probably because of this meeting place that the mark of the Sheffield Assay Office, opened in 1773, became – and still is – the crown and anchor.

At this time – the Georgian period – real silver was available only to the rich, but Bolsover's invention made it possible for the new middle classes of the early Industrial Revolution to grace their tables with Sheffield Plate at prices which were often no more than a quarter of hallmarked silver.

In 1797 the Goldsmiths' Company complained to Parliament that, 'The plated manufacturers have produced articles of the highest elegance and fashion which do material injury to the sale of wrought plate.' Such complaints did nothing to stem the flood of plated wares which now issued from the new factories in Sheffield, and from the works started in Birmingham by Matthew Boulton.

A catalogue of the 1790s lists a lidded tankard for sale at £1 10s, and a hot-water jug for £2 10s. Such prices were only a third of those for real silver articles, and when in later years the process was further perfected the prices reduced even more.

One of the difficulties in plating was to stop the thin line of copper from showing through the silver on the edges of plates and vessels. This was overcome by the invention of that rope-like edging called 'gadrooning'. In the early years the silver was fused on to one side of the copper only, and pieces which may be found like this can usually be dated up to not later than the 1760s. By the end of the eighteenth century the method of fusing silver on to both sides of a copper sheet was being copied in Paris and Vienna and as far away as St. Petersburg.

The best period for Sheffield Plate is from about 1780 to 1800 when the quality of design was so superb that even the genuine silversmiths had begun to copy it in sheer desperation.

In the earlier years the style was mainly rococo, with its familiar scrolls, ribbons and shell patterns and flowers in repoussé. In the 1760s came the neo-classical style with clear-cut curves of jugs, urns and other vessels. There were high arched handles, slender stems, and much use was made of animal heads for decoration. The growing demand for grandeur during the late eighteenth and early nineteenth centuries led to a more imposing method of styling apparent in magnificent trays and dishes piled with flowers and lion heads.

A First Book of Antiques

Among the most splendid objects made in Old Sheffield Plate are epergnes, a word which comes from the French *épargner* meaning 'to save', huge silver trays with a large central column from which sprouted branches either holding bowls of fruit or supporting hanging baskets; the tray held cruets, muffineers and so forth. The guests helped themselves and so saved the host the trouble of passing things round the table.

One difficulty which the designers had was how to cut into the thin covering of silver the heraldic symbols which the newly-rich of that period loved to have on their table-ware, especially on the trays and salvers, to impress their guests. This had to be done very carefully, sometimes by cutting away the metal and then filling the hole with silver.

The great age of Sheffield Plate lasted for a little less than a hundred years. It really came to an end in 1837 with the invention of 'British Plate' which used a mixture of copper, nickel and zinc to replace the copper sheeting. The great advantage of the new plate was that it cut the production costs as it required only one fifth of the quantity of silver used in the early years of Sheffield Plate.

Then in the 1840s Elkington invented a method by which silver was electro-plated on to Britannia Metal (a cheap alloy used by pewterers in the first half of the nineteenth century). This is known as E.P.B.M., that is Electro Plating on Britannia Metal. There is also E.P.N.S., Electro Plating on Nickel Silver.

These two methods put an end to the reign of Old Sheffield Plate, but they are liable to confuse the collector who should always ask what the base metal is when buying anything described as 'silver plate'.

4. Worcester porcelain inkstand (centre) made by Flight, Barr & Barr about 1830. First period (Dr. Wall) Worcester porcelain teacup (left) dating from about 1770 and (right) a Chamberlain Worcester mug, probably a christening mug, made about 1845. *(By courtesy of T. R. Manderson and R. W. Waite)*

5. *Below:* 18th-century Scottish flintlock pistol inlaid with silver. 17th-century German flintlock pistol inlaid with silver and wire. *(By courtesy of the Victoria and Albert Museum)*

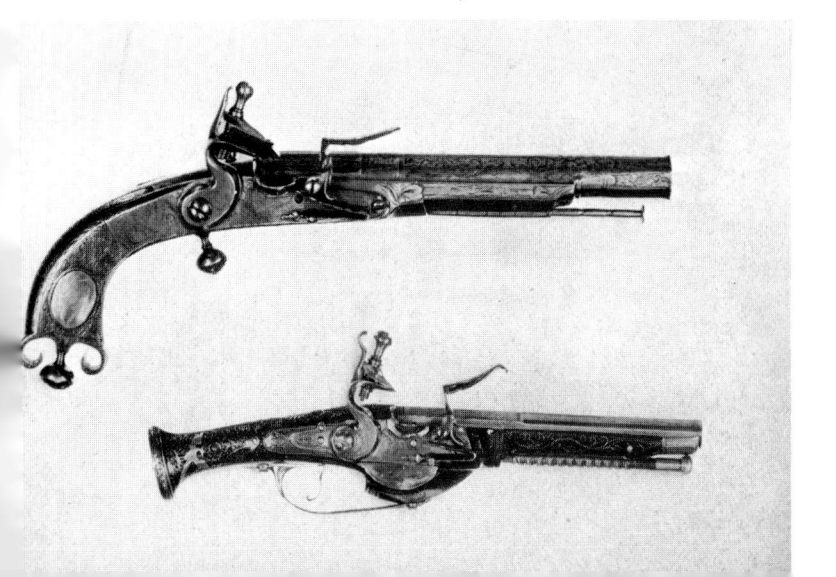

6. *Above:* Staffordshire pottery figures. Upper row, left to right, Babes in the Wood, birds' nesters, a fruit seller. Lower row, probably a pipe jar (centre) and a fisherman with his wife (left and right).
(By courtesy of T. R. Manderson)

7. *Left:* A group of Victorian brooches made of shell, glass and mother of Pearl.
(By courtesy of the Victoria and Albert Museum)

Old Sheffield Plate

E.P.B.M. is best avoided because it is a very soft metal and if anything breaks off, a handle for instance, it is very difficult to solder on again. There are few craftsmen today who can do such things. In any case, E.P.B.M. or E.P.N.S. do not have anything like the value of genuine Old Sheffield Plate.

When buying Old Sheffield Plate there are several points to watch for.

Notice whether the years have worn away some of the silver so that the copper underneath is showing through. If this is only slight it does not matter as regards the value of the piece. If there is no copper showing then draw your finger nail across the edge. If it is genuine Sheffield Plate you should be able to feel the small lip where the silver was hammered over to hide the edge of the copper.

On more important items the owners often wanted to have their initials or some heraldic crest engraved, and on these pieces the makers inserted a small plate of solid silver on which the engraving could be made. You can always detect an inserted plate by breathing on the engraving. The condensation will show up the line of the join. The same test can be used all round objects to find the line where the sheet was joined. This is more often than not under a handle.

Always clean Old Sheffield Plate with great care. Silver tarnishes easily with time and can be spoiled completely by rubbing with abrasives. Clean it only with warm water and soap it with a sponge. After that wash in warm water and dry with a very soft linen cloth. Remember to handle the piece with your fingers as little as possible.

Items in Sheffield Plate which are not difficult to find are cruets and coffee pots. Soup tureens are fairly plentiful and should be sold in pairs. Much in demand today are wine coasters which are really bottle-holders designed to protect the table from drips as a bottle was passed round.

When collecting Old Sheffield Plate remember that there are no hallmarks to guide you as with solid silver. The best course is to learn about the various periods so that you can estimate the age of a piece by its design and style.

FURTHER READING

Old Sheffield Plate by John Bedford (Cassell)
Old Sheffield Plate by R. A. Robertson (Ernest Benn)

19
Clocks

Not only can old clocks be beautiful pieces of furniture but they have the advantage of being one kind of antique which is almost impossible to fake. No one is expert enough to duplicate the intricate mechanism even if they attempt the detailed carving and painting of the case.

The earliest type of clock that is available to collectors is the sixteenth-century lantern clock. This was enclosed in a brass case designed to be placed on a bracket on the wall so that the cords and weights by which it worked could hang down through holes in the bracket.

These were replaced during the second half of the seventeenth century by the bracket clock driven not by weights but by the power of a coiled spring.

It is easy to be confused by 'bracket' and 'lantern' because it was the lantern which was placed on a bracket and should be called a bracket clock; but just to make things difficult it is not so. The earlier bracket type was called a lantern, the later one stood on a table or mantelpiece and was called a bracket! The earlier bracket clocks were often very elaborate in design, and some had a handle so that they could be carried from one room to another.

Both these types struck the hour and sometimes the quarter. Later, in the eighteenth century, many bracket clocks were made to play tunes, so they were really clocks and musical boxes combined. Sometimes the tune was played at lengthy intervals of up to every three hours, and in the more elaborate types the tune could be changed by removing the little cylinders which provided it and replacing them with different ones.

About 1660 the first grandfather or long-case clocks began to appear. These have always been the most impressive and the friendliest type to have in any room. Many people have ones which have been in the family for generations and are now worth a great deal of money, but their owners have such an affection for these great old timepieces that they will not sell them.

With their gently swaying pendulums they are the most reliable of all the old clocks. The earliest had cases – or coffins as the makers called them – of oak but these were replaced by walnut on the accession of William and Mary in 1689.

If you find a grandfather clock with no minute hand then you know it is one of the very earliest made before the second hand was added. If you find one with the name of a well-known maker carved on it, such as Thomas Tompion, James Marwick or George Graham, then you know that you have found a treasure – though the price will tell you that in any case!

On the grandfather clocks made in the Age of Walnut, that is from 1660 to 1720, the door and the surround were veneered, as was the base. This was done with what is called 'burr', or sometimes 'burl', which comes from a part of the walnut tree where the natural fibres are distorted and look like a tangled mass of twirls with dark brown spots. It has been described as looking like tangled wool. Others were

Dial hands from Long-case clocks

veneered in thin slices of wood cut from the small branches which gives the appearance of oyster shell.

Some very early walnut clocks have a circular or oval piece of thick magnifying glass set into the front at the level of the pendulum so that one gets a magnified view of the pendulum as it swings. This window was called the 'bull's eye'.

There were also walnut clocks decorated with marquetry and others coated with lacquer; but the most beautiful of all were the ones in marquetry with their floral and sunburst designs.

About the middle of the eighteenth-century mahogany took the place of walnut for the cases. Mahogany had, in fact, been used for furniture since 1720 but it was at least thirty years before the clock-makers started to use it.

Despite the beauty of the long-case clocks the aristocrats of the world of clocks are French. In 1660 there was a veritable explosion of clock-making in France and the works of art that were created during the next two centuries are among the most beautiful and sought-after objects in the whole realm of antiques.

The best engravers and goldsmiths in France worked on clocks, as did the finest cabinet-makers in the designing of the cases.

In particular it was the later years of the reign of Louis XIV, known as the Sun King (1643–1715) that saw the production of some of the most wonderfully designed and elegant clocks. The ones made then are often recognizable by the flowers and laurel wreaths in the bronze surrounds or in the woodwork itself, but the best sign of all that a clock is of the Louis XIV period is the emblem of the sun, in the form of sun rays radiating from a centre.

Bronze was used a great deal then, but in the first half of the eighteenth century rare and beautiful porcelains began to be used for the face and for ornamentations. By 1750 marble from Italy was making its appearance.

The making of these fabulous French clocks was a tightly organized business. The Paris Guild of Clockmakers which contained the élite of all these superb craftsmen, never had more than seventy-two Masters and there was always a long waiting list for members. The sons of Masters were favoured and this tended to make the Guild very much a family affair.

A few of these Masters belonged also to that small group of much envied craftsmen who were tenants of the *Galeries du Louvre* which entitled them to free lodgings and use of the finely equipped workshops in the galleries of the Louvre. At

Brass Lantern clock by John Hilderson
c. 1665

David Bouquet
1628-65

Edward East
c. 1610-73

James Rigby, early 19th Cent.

any one time there were usually three members of the Guild who enjoyed the coveted title of King's Clock-maker, in French *Horloger du Roi*.

The mechanism of French clocks tended to be much smaller than British ones. The British makers, though producing excellent timepieces, did not consider that the appearance of the inside mattered very much; the French designers attended to the appearance of everything and went in for miniaturization of the working parts. It is sometimes quite a shock to open the door of a French clock and find that the inside is mostly empty as the tiny mechanism occupies so small a part of it.

These wonders of the world of clocks are very expensive, but anybody who can afford to buy one will have not only a beautiful work of art, but an antique which is certain to increase in value year by year. There is nothing else quite like it.

FURTHER READING

Investing in Clocks & Watches by P. W. Cumhaill (Barrie & Rockcliffe)
Old Clocks by Edward Wenham (Spring Books)
Clocks and their Value by Donald de Carle (N.A.G. Press)

20
Coins

UNTIL about 2,700 years ago there were no coins. Man lived by exchange and barter. If you wanted a new axe with which to chop yourself a slice of sabre-toothed tiger you found a neighbour who had one and wanted something of yours – that tiger-skin cloak which was getting rather worn, perhaps.

As man began to live in more organized societies and make a greater variety of things this method became clumsy; he needed a means by which he could measure value, so he used objects which happened to be at hand and which varied from one country to another. Coastal tribes chose sea shells. Inland they would use stones or nuts, and in the New Hebrides feathers, probably the lightest currency ever known.

As societies grew more complex these common objects were replaced by pieces of the rarer metals such as gold and silver. Since these were so much less common than palm nuts, date stones and sea shells they were thought to have some value of their own. Soon it became inconvenient to carry about several pounds of metal so coins were made, each one having a value engraved upon it according to the weight of the metal.

The first coins so far discovered appeared in Lydia, in Asia Minor, in 700 B.C. and the idea quickly spread to the Greek city states such as Athens and Corinth. The usual emblem on those early Greek coins was the head of the Goddess of Wisdom, Pallas Athene, known later to the Romans as Minerva. But it was Philip of Macedon, father of Alexander the Great, who first used coinage on a large scale. When he captured the city of Philippi he came into possession of one of the richest gold mines in Europe and he made full use of it. Alexander later founded several mints throughout his empire which extended from Northern Greece to the borders of India. He was the first ruler to have a picture of his head engraved on a coin.

When the Romans created their first coins in the third century B.C. they bore the bearded face of Mars, God of War; a choice which seems typical of the warlike race which was destined to build an empire greater and longer lasting than Alexander's. For a long time their coins were of bronze because Italy was lacking in precious metals. The coins were large and were produced by the pound weight, hence our £ sign which comes from the Latin *libra* meaning pound.

As the legions of those small but very tough men, clad in their armour, bore the imperial eagles of Rome all over the known world, from the borders of Scotland to India in the east, from the dark forests of Germany to the deserts of North Africa in the south, so they acquired sources of gold and silver and began to use the metal for their coins. The first of these in silver were called *denarii* from which we obtain the 'd' of our £ s. d.

The large size of Roman coins enabled the die engravers to create clear designs and large portraits. The coins were changed frequently to celebrate various events. The weddings of rulers, a battle won, a new colony acquired, a forum built; all these were shown on coins which acted almost as official announcements throughout the vastness of the empire. They served also to keep the people informed of all the good things that the rulers were supposed to be doing for them, just in case they happened to forget when next they grumbled about paying some of their coins in taxes to Caesar.

When the Roman republic came to an end and the long reign of the emperors began with Augustus, nephew of the murdered Julius Caesar, their heads appeared on the coins.

There have been a thousand years of Greek and Roman coins, and in that long period the techniques of hammering blanks between dies, engraving dies and the use of portrait busts for models were all brought to a high peak of perfection.

Portrait coins are especially popular with collectors today, and there are many periods in history which produced a lot of these, from Alexander through centuries of Roman rule to the later coinage of the Byzantine Empire, produced in Constantinople, which at one time showed the head of Christ.

From the fifteenth to the eighteenth century there is a wide range of coins showing portraits of the rulers of Austria, the Tyrol and Bohemia in gold, silver and copper. But Renaissance Italy, with its independent city states, is one of the richest sources of these. Venice, Milan, Genoa and Florence all made money with the heads of their various rulers on one side. The Venetian gold *ducats* and the silver *matapanes* from the thirteenth to the sixteenth centuries spread the power and wealth of the great trading city on the Adriatic. Venetian coins showing St Mark, patron of the city, with the name of the ruling doge around him, have been found all over Europe and the Middle East.

A First Book of Antiques

Coins were first used in Britain about the first century B.C. and were primitive copies of ones then in use among the Gauls across the Channel. They were made of tin because this was almost the only metal to be found in Britain, and they usually had a picture of a bull on one side in token of the fact that breeding cattle was the main occupation of the ancient Britons.

When the Romans came they brought their own coinage along with roads, glass, central heating, and law and order. Mints were established at London and Colchester, the gold and silver being imported. And so it remained for four centuries. Early in the fifth century the last of the legions withdrew as the walls of the Empire crumbled throughout Europe under the onslaught of barbarian tribes, aided by the corruption and decay at the heart of the Empire.

Some Britons had been crying out for freedom and independence. 'Britain for the Britons!' they shouted, much as the people of Africa and Asia have shouted for the same things in more recent years. And, just as in the colonial countries of modern times, some of the natives were glad to see the Romans go, while others who had had good jobs or profited in various ways from the presence of the master race, were sorry that the old days were ended.

Then it was that the long darkness fell upon the island. With no legions to keep law and order the tribes began fighting among themselves. The roads fell into ruin and the peasant farmers made cart tracks that wound round hills and other obstacles including neighbouring farms, and so created the winding English roads of today.

In this darkness, Britain was invaded by the Saxons, Jutes and Angles from across the North Sea (England obtained its

Coins

name from the Angles who settled in the east and called their new country 'Angleland'), and there were no new coins. Life went on with a great deal of primitive exchange and barter. As the invaders settled down, however, a gold coinage began to appear showing Roman influences and also the beginnings of Anglo-Saxon art as the mixture of Angles, Jutes and Saxons merged into that new race which came to be known as the English.

The Viking invaders in the ninth century also produced coinage of their own. The hammer of Thor appears on coins minted in 921–6, and a sword on the coins of Eric 952-4, son of Harold Blue-Tooth. One coin in this period has a picture of the Minster at Winchester which was completed during the reign of Edward the Elder, 899–925.

Edgar (959–75) finally expelled the Danes and became first king of an almost united England. During his reign there were thirty-one mints producing pennies and halfpennies.

Although the invaders from Scandinavia no longer held any part of Britain they nevertheless continued to harry and plunder our eastern coasts, and Aethelred (979–1016) finally bought them off by payment of the Danegeld, a vast sum of silver coins weighing 155,000 pounds. Many have been found since in Scandinavian countries.

There were sixty mints during Aethelred's reign and the coins bear his portrait. They also show him holding a sceptre. Aethelred made the mistake of organizing a massacre of all the Danes remaining in Britain. It was a period of terror in which the soldiers of the king roamed the land seeking out and killing all the communities of Danish farmers who had settled here. When Swein, King of Denmark, heard of this, he got together a huge raiding party and invaded England in

1003, penetrating so far inland, burning and plundering in revenge, that the tales of the winged-helmeted sea-rovers spread fear throughout Britain.

He had two sons, Harold and Cnut, and after the death of Aethelred it was Cnut who became king of England and introduced on to his coinage the practice of showing the king's crowned head. Cnut is famous for two events: one being the story that he told the tide to stop coming in, and the other for having the Cheshire town of Knutsford called after him when he forded a river near it. Ford is the ancient name for a river crossing and so the town became known as Cnut's Ford.

A new foreign occupation began for Britain in 1066 when William of Normandy landed with his army and defeated King Harold at Hastings. William reigned for twenty-one years and in that time there were eight issues of pennies, all showing the King's crowned head after the fashion started by Cnut. Latin lettering showed the influence of Rome which continues even up to the present day.

In 1252 the city state of Florence created a gold coin called the *fiorino*, or florin, and this was imitated in Britain by King Henry III who ordered his goldsmith to make an issue of pure gold coin valued at 20 pence. Later, in the fourteenth century, the half florin or leopard, and the quarter florin or helm appeared. The leopard was so called because it showed the animal wearing a royal crown and mantle.

In 1489 a new gold coin called the sovereign was struck. It was worth 20s and showed King Henry VII enthroned in his robes with sceptre and orb.

In 1526 the gold 'crown of the rose' coin was minted. This showed the royal coat of arms on one side and the Tudor rose

GREEK
Silver metapontum
c. 410 B.C.

ENGLISH
gold noble, 15th Century

Commonwealth
silver crown
1653

ITALIAN
gold Florino
1252-1550

Charles II

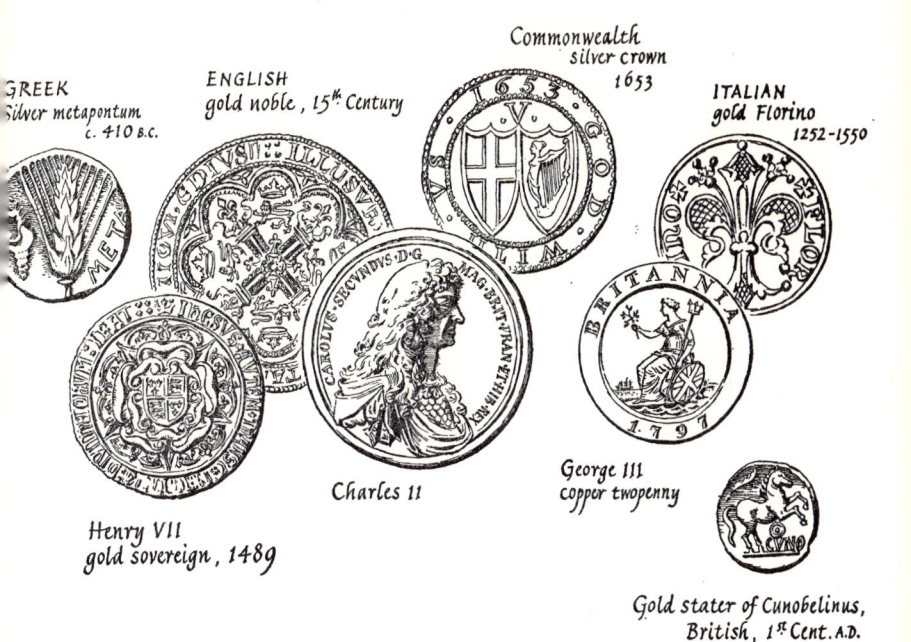

George III
copper twopenny

Henry VII
gold sovereign, 1489

Gold stater of Cunobelinus,
British, 1st Cent. A.D.

on the other. It is the origin of the crown which became worth 5s. and of the half-crown worth 2s. 6d.

The gold guinea appeared in 1662, so called because the gold of which it was made came from Guinea on the coast of Africa.

The image of Britannia had first been used on coinage as far back as A.D. 150 on Roman coins; now it reappeared in Britain in 1665 on the copper coins of Charles II. The Duchess of Richmond, a favourite of the King, posed as a model for the engraver.

There are many books which give information about the vast number of coins of other countries. There are the strange *mohurs* produced in India in the seventeenth century and which show the signs of the zodiac; and the silver *rupees* made by the British East India Company. There is the whole range of Chinese coins, and the Japanese, some of which are famous for the beautiful engraved writing.

If you want your coin collection to have any value at all it is important not to buy any old coin that you see and end up with an accumulation of many different kinds. It may look impressive to your friends but, unless you have been lucky enough to make some very unusual finds, it will be worth very little. Real coin collectors, or 'numismatists' as they are called, do not go about it in that way.

You should specialize by collecting only certain types. Make up your mind first of all what you want and ignore all others. For example, you could collect coins with certain types of animals on them, ones with pictures of armour or weapons, or those belonging to one period of one particular country. There are many different kinds from which to choose.

Your local yellow telephone directory of classified trades, which you can see at the post office or public library, will give the names and addresses of coin dealers. They will be listed either under this heading or numismatists.

Antique shops very often sell coins, but a word of warning here. This is one type of antique which it is not always a good idea to buy from an ordinary antique shop. Professional numismatists are experts who will charge you the fair and recognized trade price, whereas the average antique dealer knows a bit about everything but probably not a great deal on this subject, and he may not know the true value of the coins that he has. This means that you may sometimes pick up a real bargain when lack of knowledge about a particular

Coins

coin leads the dealer to underprice it; but obviously this takes either a lot of luck on your part or a deeper experience of coins than the dealer has, and you have not acquired that experience yet, have you? More often than not the dealer will over-price.

In London you can attend auction sales of coins which are held by a firm called Glendining's in Blenheim Street. Christie's and Sotheby's both have occasional coin auctions.

There are two vital things to bear in mind; one is that condition is just as important as age. A 300-year-old coin will not necessarily be worth a lot of money if it is very battered. You may find that a coin of 1870 is worth much more than one of 1670 if it is in what the numismatists call 'mint' condition, meaning that it has had little or no wear.

Secondly, never, never clean your old coins. This is absolutely fatal and can make them practically worthless. A lady who had read about old coins being worth much money found several dating from the beginning of the nineteenth century. She washed and polished them until they were bright and shining and then took them to a dealer. He told her that, uncleaned, he would have given her £25 for them; but as they were now he simply was not interested!

Numismatists have a language all their own, as you will see from this list of descriptions.

- F.D.C.: Perfect mint condition (the letters stand for the French 'Fleur de coin').
- UNC.: Uncirculated. This applies to *modern* coins only, which means all those minted since 1816. They must not show more than the very slightest signs of wear so that they are only a little less perfect than F.D.C.

E.F.: Extremely fine. Just a very little more worn than UNC.
V.F.: Very fine. Only slight traces of wear.
F.: Fine. Shows a definite amount of wear.
FAIR: Considerable amount of wear.
M.: Mediocre meaning very worn.
POOR: Only worth collecting at all if very rare.

There are many other descriptions such as 'Low Tide', this applies to pennies and halfpennies of 1902 on which the horizon is shown only half-way up the leg of Britannia. B.D. means beaded border, and S.H. small head. Most books on numismatics will give you a full list of these abbreviations.

Sometimes you can acquire valuable modern coins minted between 1816 and the changeover to decimal currency in February, 1971.

There is a little booklet called *All Change*, price 2s. 6d. (12·5p) which gives a complete list of modern coins and how much they are worth according to condition. Another very useful publication is the monthly magazine *Coins and Medals*.

How to keep coins? Never put them into boxes or more than one in an envelope. They scratch and batter each other and increase the effects of wear. If you cannot afford a proper coin cabinet or album you might try making a tray with holes into which to put the coins. The holes should be covered with baize or some other material so that the coins do not come into contact with the bare wood. Do not use cedar, oak or lime because these tarnish the coins after a while. Mahogany or walnut is better.

A cheaper and easier method is to put each coin into a

Coins

small plastic envelope and fasten the envelope to a board. A label can be attached giving the description.

Coin collecting has the great advantage of being relatively cheap.

FURTHER READING

Coin Collecting by Laurence Brown (Mayflower Paperback)
Coins by Elizabeth Gilzean (Corgi Mini-Book)
Treasury of the World's Coin by F. Reinfield (Oak Tree Press)

21

Victorian Jewellery

AT any antique fair or dealer's shop you are almost certain to find a tray or glass cabinet of sparkling jewellery from the Victorian era. They are among the easiest of antiques to collect and include an infinite variety of items which never fail to interest.

Victorian jewellery reflects the changes of fashion during most of the nineteenth century when the Industrial Revolution was in full swing and the modern world as we know it was being formed.

Women have always loved to adorn themselves with bangles and baubles, and the craft of jewellery-making is one of mankind's oldest activities.

Until the end of the seventeenth century the method of cutting diamonds, always the most popular of precious stones, was crude; the set and ornamentation were the most important aspects of jewellery-making. But at the end of the century two new methods of cutting were developed. One of these was called the 'brilliant cut' and the other the 'rose cut'. The rose cut diamond is covered with twenty-four triangular facets in the shape of a hemisphere with a flat base. It produces a soft brilliance, though not so alive and sparkling as the brilliant cut. This new technique advanced slowly throughout the eighteenth century.

It was not until the new prosperity of the machine age that

Victorian Jewellery

a piece of jewellery could become anything more than a very expensive gift from one wealthy aristocrat to another. Society underwent a considerable change as the Victorian age began and the new manufacturing industries created a prosperous middle-class which could afford to adorn its women with precious stones. As the century advanced even the ordinary working people could buy more with the wages which they earned in the factories, and could afford, not, of course, expensive gems, but at least imitation jewellery made of a kind of paste or perhaps of lava stone.

The Victorians were a very sentimental people, much more so than we are, and they loved to keep locks of hair of loved ones woven into precious gems from which brooches, bracelets and ear-rings were made. They also carried tiny portraits in miniature clasps either on bracelets or serving as the centres of brooches. When a couple became engaged it was customary – for those who could afford it – to have the girl's portrait framed in pearls for the man to wear attached to his watch chain. His portrait would be framed in either pearls or diamonds and worn by the girl as a locket.

The Victorians also believed in a great deal of mourning. When a man died his widow would have to wear black clothes for a very long time, and the only jewellery allowed in such periods was that made of jet, which is a kind of very black anthracite coal, only it does not dirty the hands as coal does and can be very highly polished. Queen Victoria, who seemed to be almost always in mourning for some member of the royal family, helped to set the fashion for jet. So great was the demand for it that it became the major industry of the Yorkshire town of Whitby where there were rich deposits of the material. From France an imitation jet was imported for those who could not afford the real thing. This was simply black glass.

In the 1830s fashion dictated that a woman's head and neck should be highlighted by low-cut dresses, so the tiara became popular, as did the custom of wearing a pendent jewel on the forehead. Necklaces, lockets, and long ear-rings descending towards bare shoulders all became fashionable.

But in the next decade necklines were worn high and ears were covered by either hair or bonnets; ear-rings were consequently out of fashion and hands became the centre of attention. Bracelets and rings were the main items of jewellery. In the 1850s ear-rings were in again but smaller than before; large brooches were worn at the throat and in the evenings elaborate necklaces were all the rage.

By the 1860s the crinoline, which had come into fashion towards the end of the previous decade, was well established and the heavy velvet materials that were worn called for heavy jewellery. Colours were consequently bright and much use was made of coloured stones such as amethyst and topaz. Brooches, necklaces and bracelets were heavy and elaborately decorated.

As the century progressed dress was noted for its many bows and braids. Ears were uncovered and there were gold fringes on the ear-rings; pendants were large and on lockets every bit of the gold setting was decorated. But in the 1880s dresses became straight and simple, adorned only by plain strings of amber beads or heavy chains. In the evenings small diamonds and plain gold bangles were worn.

This fashion did not last long, however, for in the 1890s – for the first time in decades – women wore feminine clothes: swishing petticoats, and dresses which outlined their curves.

Victorian Jewellery

Lace became very popular and jewellery tended to be smaller and lighter. Bracelets had to be narrow or women were hopelessly out of fashion. There were pins instead of brooches; ear-rings became just the tiniest studs and the smallest diamonds were preferred, usually a lot of them to give a scintillating effect like a galaxy. And so the Victorian age drew to its close with women emphasizing their figures and glittering like the sky at night.

One particular fashion which lasted throughout the century and was able to survive the changes was that of the *parure*, a set of matching jewels which could include ear-rings, necklaces, bracelets and several other ornaments.

In the previous century there had been an obsession with copying the classical motifs found in the newly-excavated ruins of Pompeii and Herculaneum. We have seen in the chapter on Wedgwood how this affected the design of pottery, and in the Victorian age this classicism enjoyed a revival which lasted throughout the century.

The latter half of the nineteenth century was a great period of archaeological excavation and discovery in Egypt and the Middle East generally, and the Victorian middle-class, with its keen desire for education, developed a liking for jewellery in the fashions of bygone ages. Some famous firms made items in the styles of ancient Rome, Greece, Egypt, Assyria and, in fact, of almost every country and period. In 1876 the Queen officially became Empress of India and this led to a vogue for Oriental designs.

Another event which had a strong influence was the series of excavations made by the German, Dr Schliemann, on the site of Troy in Asia Minor. Jewellery was made with designs based on those found on vases and other ornaments that were dug up. Greek mottoes of love were inscribed on bracelets and lockets.

Two famous designers exerted a great influence in applying the classical motif to jewellery. One of these was Castellani of Rome and the other Giulliano of London.

Castellani was interested in the cult of Roman designs based on the discoveries which the French archaeologists had made at Pompeii, but he also looked beyond the Roman. He believed that the Romans had not been truly original designers but had obtained their inspiration from other people before them – and he proved to be right.

In 1815 Castellani heard that in the little villages in the remote hills of Umbria there were craftsmen working in gold and using methods and designs which had not changed for centuries. He investigated and found that these men were using very fine granulated gold in a manner which even the Romans had never known He concluded that this was Etruscan work, the art of the little-known race which had inhabited Italy when Rome itself was no more than a fishing village on the Tiber. He brought some of them to work for him in Rome where they produced what came to be called the Etruscan filigree style. This art, which began in the dawn of recorded history, came to dominate the fashionable salons of the nineteenth century.

As the century progressed, however, and the middle-classes became more prosperous, the demand grew for jewellery which, though based upon the designs of artists such as Castellani, was nevertheless made of stones less expensive than the big four: diamonds, emeralds, rubies and sapphires which are classed as the 'precious' stones. The demand was met by the growth of an industry producing jewels in the semi-precious stones such as amethyst, topaz, opal, garnet and several others; it is mostly this jewellery which can be found today in the fairs and shops of the antique dealers.

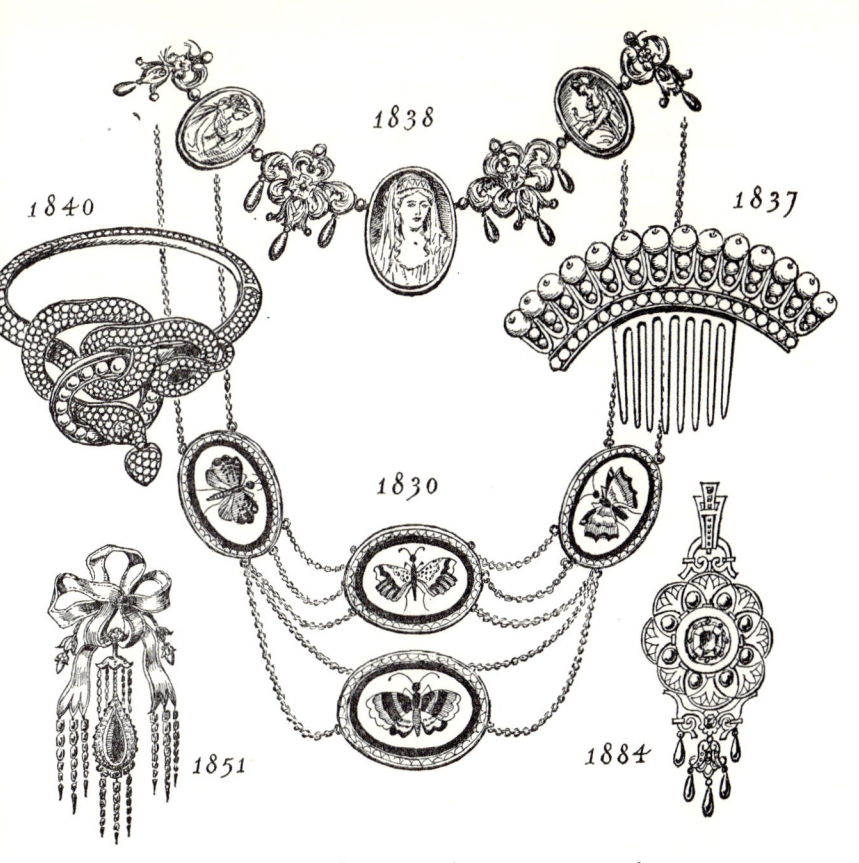

A large part of the British business consisted of exports to South America to the Latin races who have always loved very colourful adornments, and this resulted in the creation of jewellery using the semi-precious stones arranged in exotic colourings.

The discovery of rich opal mines in Australia furthered the production of this jewellery. Opals had been known in the ancient world where the Roman writer, Pliny, had written

[109]

A First Book of Antiques

that, 'In them you shall see the living fire of the ruby, the glorious purple of the amethyst, the green sea of the emerald; all glittering together in an incredible mixture of light.'

Wide uses were found for the opal, especially to form the body of a bird or butterfly in a brooch where its only fault lay in the fact that, unlike any other stone, it was liable to contract or expand slightly according to temperature, so that stones could get lost.

With jewels such as the opal, however, and the amethyst with its facets cut on an inclined plain to bring out its purple to lilac colouring, it is not surprising that craftsmen were able to produce superb substitutes for the precious four.

Here is a list of the semi-precious stones most commonly used by the Victorian jeweller.

Agate: Most popular in brooches, usually dyed before being fixed in the setting.

Alexandrite: Named after Alexander II of Russia. Shows different colours according to angle of view.

Amber: This is the petrified resin of trees which grew millions of years ago. Used in necklaces and rings.

Amethyst: Used in many types of jewellery. At its best when set in gold.

Aquamarine: Varies from pale blue to green.

Bloodstone: Dark green with spots of red.

Coral: The skeleton of a marine polyp.

Garnet: Green but there is also a deep-red variety.

Jade: Used especially for ear-rings. The clear green variety was found best for necklaces.

Lapis Lazuli: A deep blue stone known and used for jewellery in ancient Egypt.

Onyx: A quartz used for brooches and bracelets.

Victorian Jewellery

Opal: As already described.

Peridot: Varies from yellow to green.

Spinel: A stone with a very wide range of colour from red and yellow to blue. Mostly used in rings.

Topaz: Found in blue, pink and rich brown. One of the most popular and beautiful of all the Victorian gems.

Turquoise: A blue stone often found in brooches and bracelets.

Tourmaline: Almost unique in sometimes having red and green in the same stone.

Zircon: A brown stone.

Both gold and rolled gold, which consisted of thin plates of gold fused on to common metal rather like the silver for Sheffield Plate, were used a great deal.

Cameos made from mollusc shells were skilfully carved and often set in gold; and after 1860 there are cameos made from lava which has a cold rubbery feel.

At one period there was a fashion for Scottish products such as Cairngorm brooches, jewelled dirks, ram's head snuff-boxes and Scottish emblems set in pearls taken from the rivers of Scotland.

There has never been an age so jewellery-conscious as the Victorian. It was an age which was drab and ugly with the smoke and dirt of the new factories and the sprawling, unplanned cities that were shooting up as the machine age expanded. The people had to have something with which to brighten their surroundings, and especially to bring a sparkle to their clothes, for some of the fashions of the age were among the ugliest of any period in history. Jewellery served to lighten the effect of heavy fabrics and sombre colours.

Carved Ivory broach, 1860

Today the beautiful objects which the Victorian jewellers created are available in their infinite variety of types, designs and materials, from the fantastically expensive to the quite cheap.

FURTHER READING

Jewellery 1837–1901 by Margaret Flower (Cassell)
English Victorian Jewellery by Ernie Bradford (Country Life).

22

Glass Paperweights

THE best of glass paperweights are among the most beautiful objects in all the world of antiques, yet they are fairly recent, dating only from 1845. They depend for their magical and colourful effect upon an invention which dates back to ancient times in Egypt – the invention of *millefiori*, meaning, in Italian, a thousand flowers.

In the Nile Valley, at least some hundreds of years B.C., the Egyptian glass-blowers developed the art of placing together a number of blobs of different-coloured glass and heating them until the entire mass fused. They were careful not to raise the heat so much that the colours mingled. Then the mass was drawn out, slowly and cautiously, into long canes.

The trick was used for the decoration of vases and other items, and later the Romans took over the idea; not that they were ever a very artistic people, being much handier with the sword and the law book, but they were never averse to using the ideas of those whom they considered barbarians.

In the course of time the grandeur of Rome that had seemed eternal passed away, leaving the legacy of its roads, the classic columns that had fronted its temples and forums, the framework of its laws – and its language destined to be taught in the public schools of another empire that lay in the far distant future. The Dark Ages fell upon Europe as the barbarian hordes swarmed in over the walls of empire bringing with them the darkness of the forests from which they came.

Time passed. Slowly, Europe emerged from the darkness and in the Middle Ages in the Mediterranean region great city states arose and grew prosperous and wealthy on trade with distant lands. Such a one – most powerful of them all – was Venice, 'Queen of the Adriatic'. To enrich that city came the artists and craftsmen of many races; and one of the products for which Venice became famous was glass.

On the island of Murano in the Venetian lagoon, closely guarded from jealous rivals, the glassworks whose fame spread throughout the known world, developed.

In 1495 Marco Antonio Sabellico, librarian of the basilica of St Mark and historian of Venice, wrote a book about the Murano glassworks in which he referred to 'a famous invention first proved that glass might feign the whiteness of crystal, and they began to turn the material into various colours and numberless forms – but consider to whom did it first occur to include in a little ball all the arts of flowers which clothe the meadows in spring?'

To whom indeed? No one knew, but, although the Venetian glass-makers on their tight little island made some use of the art of millefiori to simulate myriads of tightly packed little flowers, it was still to be a very long time before anyone thought of using the idea in paperweights. In fact, there wasn't much call for paperweights in a world in which few people could read and write.

Not until 1845 did a Venetian artist named Pierre Bigaglia make the first true paperweights with the sparkling jewel-like millefiori imprisoned inside. He exhibited a number of them at the Austrian Industrial Fair in Vienna where they

Glass Paperweights

excited great curiosity. One person who became very interested was a French professor named Eugene Peligot. He bought several and took them back to Paris. By the following year they were being copied by three French glass factories. One of these factories was at Clichy, near Paris; and the other two were at Baccarat and St Louis, both in the Vosges mountains. The St Louis factory was especially lucky in being in a region of fine sand and many trees which provided wood for fuel.

For some unknown reason Venice missed the opportunity. The invention of Pierre Bigaglia was never taken up at Murano, perhaps because the famed island of glass had long passed its peak. It was the French who developed the production of glass paperweights together with some competition from glassworks in Bohemia.

Each factory tended to have its own range of colours and designs. Some items are marked and the most famous mark on any paperweight is the rose used by the Clichy factory.

For a decade there was a rage for these extraordinary and unique creations; then, by 1860, it was all over. The fad died and they were forgotten – until 1920 when a certain H. W. L. Way wrote an article for a magazine in which he described a collection of French millefiori weights which he had started in 1912. This article began the new fashion of collecting glass paperweights and today they are among the most treasured of collectors' items, some of the rarer ones selling at auctions for several thousands of pounds.

One famous collection was that of a Mr Z. Djeva of Paris who began when he was a boy of thirteen. In 1922 he paid £100 for a rare Clichy weight, and in later years refused an offer of £7,000 for it!

The late King Farouk of Egypt was another avid collector. He began in 1940 and had agents and dealers all over the world buying wherever they could find the rarest and most beautiful examples. By 1952, when the Egyptian army revolted and he had to flee from his palace, Farouk had amassed what was probably the world's biggest collection which now belongs to the Egyptian nation.

When looking for millefiori paperweights one should be careful not to be deceived by the modern ones which are

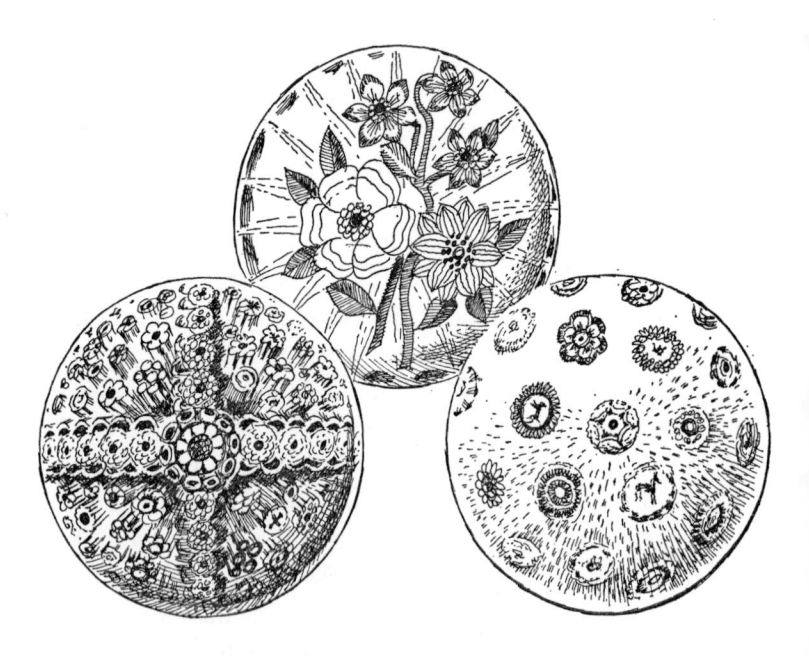

being produced today in Britain and America. Many are made at a factory in Wealdstone and some extremely good ones come from Scotland, where a Spanish immigrant named Ysart started a business. There was even a period in

Glass Paperweights

the 1930s when American dealers sent old weights to China to be copied by Chinese glass-blowers.

To see exactly what the genuine old ones look like one should study them in museums, especially the collection in the Victoria and Albert.

FURTHER READING

Paperweights by John Bedford (Cassell)
Paperweights & other Glass Curiosities by E. M. Elville (Country Life)

23
Toys

TOYS seem always to have been with us, perhaps even in ancient Egypt.

Pieces of miniature furniture have been dug up in the Nile Valley and some experts believe that these may have occupied the earliest dolls' houses. In Britain a tiny chair and sofa made of lead were found in the ruins of a Roman villa dated A.D. 100.

Toys are eagerly sought by collectors, the contents of dolls' houses from Holland and Germany being among the most popular items.

The Dutch dolls' houses of the seventeenth century were splendid affairs and the expensive ones contained furniture of solid silver, every item of which was hallmarked, even the tiny thimbles and bodkins in jewelled sewing-boxes. In the kitchens were frying-pans with realistic silver fishes in them.

In Windsor Castle one of the most elaborate dolls' houses ever made in Britain can be seen. This was designed by the famous architect Sir Edwin Lutyens, and measures 8 feet 4 inches in length. It has models of 1924 Rolls-Royce cars in the garage and water gushes from the silver taps into the bath with its mother-of-pearl floor.

Complete dolls' houses, however, are difficult to find in antique shops. In modern times dealers have broken them up and sold their contents separately, so it is the aim of collectors to acquire complete sets of furnishings, and these can be found in many different materials.

Thomas Whieldon made tiny tea sets in a colour-blending earthenware, also teapots with a so-called tortoise-shell glaze. Wedgwood and Davenport made watering cans and flowerpots which were really sold more for decoration as mantelpiece ornaments than for the inside of dolls' houses. In the 1850s one London firm of toy makers produced 5,000 tiny copper kettles a year which sold at 6d. each.

In 1920 the collecting of dolls became popular and these are eagerly sought today. Mostly the ones that can be found were made in the nineteenth century when they began to be turned out commercially. The first came from Germany and were made of papier-mâché. These were rigid and without any joints, so their limbs did not move at all.

Germany produced wooden dolls with ball and socket joints in the 1820s. Often these were quite big, even up to 40 inches in height; some excellent ones can be seen in the London Museum.

In the 1840s wax dolls with wax-coated papier-mâché heads were manufactured. The design of these was usually simple and the modelling crude. Sometimes they had glass eyes moved by wires and bodies stuffed with calico.

China-headed dolls, some of them made in Meissen porcelain, appeared at the end of the decade. It is surprising that such beautiful objects as these were made to play with, and even more surprising that many have survived through the years. In fact they were still being made up to 1914.

In the early 1850s some very expensive dolls were made of thick poured wax which made them look very natural. They had real hair, eyebrows and eyelashes, set into the wax with great skill. They first attracted attention when they were shown in London at the Great Exhibition of 1851. A disadvantage of these dolls was that if they were left near a fire or even outside in hot sun they would melt.

The famous French Fashion Dolls arrived on the scene a few years later. The aristocrats of the doll world for the next thirty years, these had swivelling heads of porcelain or biscuit. The Fashion Dolls had many different bodies, some wooden with movable joints, some jointed metal and others of firmly-stitched kid. Their heads had fine wigs and very elaborate *coiffures*.

In Paris there were even fashion houses for them where they were dressed in furs, stockings, gloves, jewels and handbags. Some were even provided with ornamented trunks for accessories and changes of clothes and wigs. The French dress salons were at one time accused of exporting the dolls as advertisements for Paris fashions. These elegant and beautiful dolls were called *poupées*, and in the 1880s came a variation of them called *bébés* which had hollow limbs and joints strung on tight elastic. Their large, lustrous eyes could even cry. They walked, talked and some were musical.

It is believed that Roman children probably played with toy soldiers made of wood, but whether they were really toys or ornaments, perhaps of a semi-religious nature, is not known for certain. We do know, however, that German toy-makers were carving toy soldiers out of wood in the nineteenth century.

For a long time toy soldiers were also made out of block tin but it was not until 1893 that a man named William Britain made model Life Guards out of semi-solid lead, and this was the start of the lead soldiers as we know them today.

*Victorian china dolls, 5½" high
c. 1860*

A First Book of Antiques

These, however, are a little too recent to be classed as antique.

More collectable are the little wooden animals that went into the toy arks made during the middle years of the nineteenth century. The arks themselves are as difficult to find as complete dolls' houses and for the same reason: they have mostly been broken up; but the animals can still be found

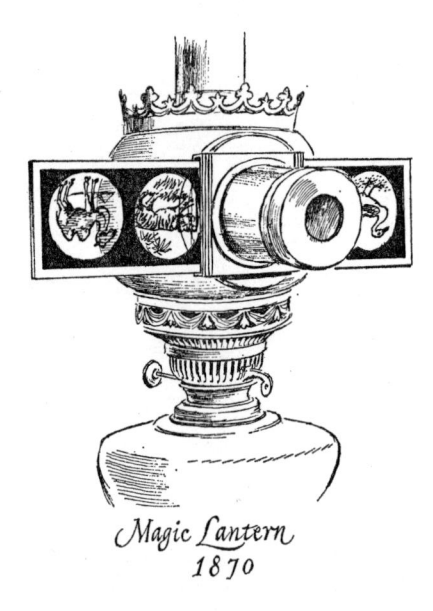

Magic Lantern
1870

and collectors aim to acquire as complete a set in pairs as possible. These can amount to quite a lot. There were some Victorian arks containing as many as 400!

In the 'bad old days' of Victorian England children were often employed under appalling conditions to make toys. In 1842 a report on the Employment of Children in Factories quoted a boy of nine who told the investigators that, 'I work from dawn to dusk and can make forty dozen toys in a day.

Toys

I am paid a penny for every ten dozen!' These were small toys which were sold in the streets at a penny each.

The toys that these exploited children made are now sought by collectors in junk and antique shops today.

FURTHER READING

A History of Dolls' Houses by Flora Gill Jacobs (Cassell)
History of Toys by Antonia Fraser (Weidenfeld & Nicolson)

24
How and Where to Buy Antiques

Antiques can be bought at the following places:
Antique shops
Junk shops
Antique fairs
Auction sales
Street Markets
Through advertisements in newspapers and magazines
We shall look at these one at a time.

Antique shops When you go into one of these there is one most important thing to bear in mind: *don't break anything!*

There will sometimes be notices telling you that 'If you break it you've bought it!' It is not a good idea to start your career as an antique collector by carelessly sweeping your coat or waving an arm and smashing to the floor a piece of seventeenth-century Meissen porcelain. Imagine yourself staring down with horror at the bits round your feet, and especially at the price tag lying there looking up at you – £350! So be careful – you have been warned!

Most dealers don't like you to handle things at all, but if you should at any time pick up an antique do it as the professionals do: use both hands. *Never* pick up a breakable article with one hand only.

How and Where to Buy Antiques

Most items in antique shops are marked with the price. When an item is not marked it usually means that the owner is prepared to bargain, but it would be a mistake for you to make an offer.

If the owner or attendant should say, 'How much would you like to offer?' always refuse very firmly to suggest any figure because the chances are that whatever price you think of, it will be more than he is expecting. You must insist that he names a figure. It it turns out to be less than you thought then you might accept, but otherwise you can bargain. Never pretend to be well off. Shake your head sadly and say that you cannot go so high but add that you might be able to pay, say, three quarters of what he asks. Three times out of four you will walk out of that shop having bought the item for a lower figure.

Bargains can sometimes be obtained in antique shops. Very often the people who run them are dealers with years of experience who can tell at a glance whether a chair is in the Chippendale style or whether a Staffordshire figure is chemically crazed or genuinely old, but so vast is the world of antiques that even the most experienced dealers do not know everything.

In one shop a collector picked up a rather curious object. Made of Chinese porcelain it was a figure of a woman lying on a couch. It was not very artistic, not even well painted. The price was £5. When the collector asked the owner if he knew what it was, he replied that it was just a figure, without any special meaning.

The collector bought that figure and shortly afterwards sold it to another dealer for £50! You see, he knew what the owner of the shop did not know, that the object was what is

A First Book of Antiques

called a 'medicine figure'. In ancient China it was not the right thing for male doctors to examine women patients, so when a woman went to a doctor he brought out the medicine figure, she pointed to the part where she had a pain and the doctor would make a guess at what the complaint might be and treat his patient accordingly. Such figures are rare.

With experience you should be able in time to know when an item is worth more than the dealer is asking. It is not your business to tell him what he does not know.

Never buy an antique without asking for a note stating that the item is as described. For example, if you have bought a piece of silver the guarantee note should state that it is genuine Sterling silver of a certain period. It should also give the designer's name if known. If you should find out within one month that the item is a fake or not what you were led to believe when you bought it, then you are entitled to claim your money back.

Another point which many customers do not know is that if you have bought two items and see a third that you would like, then most reputable dealers will give you a reduction on the third one. Some may not tell you about this and in that case you should mention it. This applies, of course, only to three items bought during the *same* visit.

Junk shops A householder who recently put out with his dust-bin a cardboard box containing a number of old and unwanted ornaments was surprised to see the dust-man, instead of emptying it into the vehicle, place the box in the driver's cab. That dust-man was one of many who have heard of the great antiques boom. He knew that people often throw away objects which they think are rubbish but which can be sold today at a profit. Some of those ornaments would

How and Where to Buy Antiques

find their way to a junk shop and the dust-man would be the richer by anything up to a few pounds depending on his luck.

The pickings are especially rich in slum clearance areas: Victorian door knockers in the shape of an animal head, or perhaps a hand grasping a bar; copper or brass hearth ornaments, bronze shepherdesses and archers which can be made attractive by gilding. Many such things are being thrown away with the rubble of old houses as they are knocked down. The owners often do not know that when junk becomes old enough and rare enough it also becomes antique.

These throw-outs can be found in the junk shops rather than in antique shops. A lot of it will be rubbish, but sometimes you will find items worth more than the owner of the shop realizes. After all, he is not an antique dealer and his knowledge is usually much more limited.

Look especially for furniture. Do not expect to find a painting by Van Gogh or an undiscovered Gauguin. You would not recognize it anyway, would you? Paintings are strictly for the experts.

Antique fairs There are nearly thirty of these every year in various towns such as Manchester, Buxton, Brighton, Southport, Harrogate, Cambridge and others. There is also the well-known one in Chelsea.

The fairs usually last for a week and are advertised in advance in the monthly magazine *The Collectors Guide*. Everything on view at an antiques fair is for sale and the same rules apply as in shops. You will find, however, that since dealers themselves come to buy at fairs the level of prices tends to be higher than in the shops.

A fair saves you some travelling because you have the

equivalent of thirty or forty shops all together in one big hall. It is also a wonderful opportunity to gain experience by seeing such a treasure trove of antiques in one place.

A warning: do not go to a fair during the last two or three hours of the final day, you will find many stall-holders packing their things away.

Auction sales The most famous of these are Sotheby's and Christie's in London; and of the two it is Sotheby's who can claim to be the oldest art auctioneers in the world.

In 1744 a man named Samuel Baker, of Covent Garden, held a sale of art objects and old books in public, and founded the firm which came to be known as Sotheby's. The practice of holding public art auctions came from Holland where it was started in the early seventeenth century, but it was Samuel Baker who built the firm that has lasted longer than any other. Many people have gone into the same kind of business at various times but most of them have crashed.

Among famous sales at Sotheby's was that of a private collection of books called the Britwell Library which went to an American bidder for $3 million. Another was the sale of a picture by Cézanne for £220,000 in 1954, and in 1964 a Louis XV commode sold for £63,000.

Christie's began in 1766 when a young man named James Christie held his first public auction. Christie was a gifted speaker and was known as 'The Specious Orator'. He would begin a sale with, 'Let me entreat you, ladies and gentlemen, permit me to put this inestimable piece of elegance under your protection. Your inexhaustible and candid generosity must harmonize with the brilliance of this little jewel!'

Very different is the modern auctioneer at Christie's with his crisp 'Lot 51, £15,000, thank you!'

How and Where to Buy Antiques

One of Christie's most spectacular sales in recent times was that of a Louis XV silver tureen which sold for £45,000; on another occasion a picture by the French painter Claude Monet established a European record by selling for £588,000!

London is the world's major art centre. Often antiques are sent from America to be auctioned at Sotheby's or Christie's where they are bought by Americans and so go right back!

However, if you do not live in London there are many other leading auctioneers throughout the country. Their sales are advertised in local newspapers, and may include country house sales at which the contents of a large house are auctioned.

At a sale nothing has a price on it. All the items are sold to the person who bids the highest. It is a good idea to go along beforehand – usually the previous day – when the items to be sold are on view and you can examine them freely.

If you bid the first time you go to an auction sale you may land yourself in trouble through lack of experience. You may also make a fool of yourself by bidding £2 for a Sheraton table which eventually sells for £200! And worse things than that can happen ... It is no good looking amazed when the auctioneer points to you and announces that you have just bought a Louis XIV clock for £500 because he thought that your nervous twitch was a signal to double the last price offered!

If you suffer from nervous twitches perhaps you should stay away from auction sales, at first, anyway. Better to look round for a friendly attendant on the day before and ask him to bid for you. Tell him what you want and how much you are prepared to pay. Make sure he understands that he must not carry the bidding above your top figure. If he succeeds you give him a suitable tip, say 5 per cent.

A job lot is often a good thing to bid for. It will contain a number of items some of which will be of little or no value, but sometimes you can find a modest treasure among them.

Street markets Many towns have markets in which antiques are sold, the most famous being London's Portobello Road. You need to be extra careful, however. In the Portobello Road, for example, many stalls are run by professional dealers who do this as a sideline with a shop elsewhere, so that buying from them is really much the same as in a shop.

But an increasing number of stalls now are run by art students and housewives who have a lot of enthusiasm but limited knowledge. They are likely sometimes to buy fakes or rubbish which they think is genuine. This means that you can be deceived if you believe that the person selling them is an expert.

The best bargains in markets are sold very early in the day, during the first hour, because this is the time when dealers come and buy, often sweeping the place clean of the day's prize pieces. But you, too, can get up early!

Advertisements in newspapers and magazines It is often very useful to keep an eye on such advertisements in case you see something for which you have been searching: an engraved Bowie Knife to complete your collection of daggers, or an addition to that collection of Arabian coins which you started. You can also place advertisements yourself when you want to sell something, or even when you want items. This way you may obtain pieces which otherwise it could take you years to find.

A very useful organization to join is the Antique Collect-

How and Where to Buy Antiques

ors' Club. This was formed in 1966 and has local branches in many towns. If there is one in your area you can attend its regular meetings and listen to lectures and discussions, besides talking to fellow collectors. The branches also organize visits to museums, auction sales, exhibitions and so forth. There is no minimum age for becoming a member.

The club publishes a monthly magazine in which you can advertise. You can also obtain books at reduced prices. The address is Clopton, Woodbridge, Suffolk.

However you go about buying always beware of the swings of fashion. Often some particular kind of antique will become fashionable. Collectors will be eager to purchase and prices shoot up; but unless you are buying with the idea of selling again soon you may find that the ceiling has suddenly been reached. The fashion fades as quickly as it began and prices fall. A few years ago there was a fashion for collecting old books. People who bought and hung on to them can now get only about a third of the price which they originally paid.

Rember also to try to build up *collections*. For example: if you want Wedgwood try to acquire a tea-set in one material, say green Jasper or cream ware, making sure that each piece is of the same period.

Another idea would be a collection of Wedgwood commemorative mugs, that is ones made to celebrate famous events such as Queen Victoria's coronation, the Battle of Waterloo, the 1851 Exhibition in Hyde Park and so forth. Or, if you collect silver, stick to one craftsman, one period, or one type of article such as spoons, teapots, paper-knives, etc.

When collecting furniture always bear in mind that a lot of it was made for big rooms in the houses of the wealthy. It is no use bidding at an auction sale for a big Welsh dresser if you live in a council house!

In everything to do with antiques always remember the Latin motto of the wise collector: *Caveat emptor* (buyer beware). There are many things to beware of, particularly when there may be fakes or forgeries. A fake, according to the dictionary, is something tampered with, made to 'deceive, defraud, cheat', while a forgery is something made to imitate a genuine article, 'a fraudulent deception'.

A Staffordshire ware figure made in the 1960s and chemically crazed so that it seems to be 150 years old is thus a forgery. A Chippendale chair the legs of which have been broken off and on to which new legs have been fastened, then painted and stained to look like the old, is a fake.

Nothing is easier to forge than ceramics, and it is not only individuals who do it. In the past even quite reputable firms were not above putting the marks of other companies on their own wares. Many thousands of pieces bearing the crossed swords of Meissen were made in England or France or various parts of Germany. An item of silver may have been broken and new pieces cunningly soldered on so that the value is greatly reduced when you come to sell it to someone who discovers the alteration. The mark can have been tampered with, too, to make the piece seem older than it is.

A few useful points to remember are:

1 The word 'England' on pottery and porcelain only appears after 1891, although it is worth noting that there

How and Where to Buy Antiques

were just a few firms using it from 1880; but in either case such items are not old enough to classify as antiques.
2 'Made in England' only appears after 1900. Such items are not antiques.
3 'Limited' or simply "Ld" appears after 1860 so only the very earliest of such items are antiques.
4 'Trade Mark' began to be used when the Trade Marks Act came into force in 1862 but not until after 1875 did this mark come into common use.
5 Date marks included with a maker's mark almost always mean the date when the firm was founded, not the date of manufacture of the item.
6 'Royal' only appears after about 1850.

The study of antiques is the study of the history of art and culture. The designs of ceramics, furniture, silver, glass, etc., reflect the changing tastes and fashions which are due to the changes of an evolving society. The tides of history, of battles, revolutions and migrations can be traced in the many and varied aspects of the fascinating world of antiques.

Too many people in the business today are collecting and selling for profit and nothing else. Hard-faced dealers regard a vase of precious Chinese porcelain as nothing more than a piece of goods on which to make a profit. They have no interest in the 1,000 years of history behind that object of beauty, created so lovingly by a long-dead potter, painted with care and skill by an artist famous in his day.

There is no reason why one should not buy and sometimes sell an antique at a profit in order to buy more, and it is always useful to own something which is an investment as well as a thing of beauty. But the main purpose of collecting antiques should be for the love of that which is old, rare and beautiful and which mirrors the history of mankind. Too often art is degraded by the profit-makers into just another money-making business.

Antiques can be collected in your home town or on holiday; wherever you go there are antique and junk shops yielding unexpected treasures; and there is the thrill of suddenly finding that thirteenth Apostle Spoon to complete your collection, or another William and Mary coin for your tray.

Happy collecting!

Glossary of terms used in this book

Ball and Claw Foot: The foot of a table, chair or cabinet in the shape of an animal's paw (usually a lion's) extended over a ball. Chippendale used this a lot.

Biscuit: A piece of pottery or porcelain which has been left in the unglazed state.

Cabriole Leg: A curved leg used almost universally on furniture throughout the eighteenth century.

Chinoiserie: Any type of decoration based on Chinese designs. Used in furniture, pottery, porcelain, glass, etc.

Commode: Chest of drawers, chiffonier.

Filigree: A fine, delicate tracery of ornamental work in gold or silver wire. Mostly used in jewellery.

Gadrooning: A type of decoration on the edges of silver ware, pottery and porcelain or furniture. Looks a bit like twisted rope.

Marquetry: A method of decorating furniture by covering it with thin plates of wood of different colours and contrasting grains.

Neo-Classical: Designs based on those of ancient Greece and Rome. Became popular following the excavations at Pompeii and Herculaneum in the eighteenth century.

Papier-Mâché: A material made with layers of pulped paper soaked in a mixture of chalk, flour and glue which is compressed and then heated. Usually lacquered afterwards.

Repoussé: A method of putting a design on to silver by hammering, or embossing, from the *inside*. The opposite of engraving, which is done from the outside.

Rococo: A style of decoration which came into use in the seventeenth century and consists of flowing lines based on scrolls and the patterns of shells.

Splats: The central, upright portion of a chair back.

GENERAL FURTHER READING

Small Antiques for the Collector by D. C. Gohm (John Gifford)

Antique China & Glass under £5 by Geoffrey A. Godden (Arthur Barker)

Collecting Cheap China & Glass by Guy Williams (A Corgi Mini-Book)

Antiques in their Periods by Hampden Gordon (John Murray)

Buying Antiques by Coysh & King (David & Charles)

A Pocket Guide to the Marks of Origin on British and Irish Silver Plate by Frederick Bradbury (J. W. Northend, Sheffield)

Pocket Book of English Ceramic Marks by J. P. Cushion (Faber & Faber)

The Antique Periods

		reign of
TUDOR	1485–1558	HENRY VII / HENRY VIII / EDWARD VI / MARY
ELIZABETHAN	1558–1603	ELIZABETH I
JACOBEAN	1603–1649	JAMES I / CHARLES I
COMMONWEALTH	1649–1659	CROMWELL
RESTORATION	1660–1689	CHARLES II / JAMES II
WILLIAM AND MARY	1689–1702	WILLIAM AND MARY
QUEEN ANNE	1702–1714	QUEEN ANNE
GEORGIAN	1714–1820	GEORGE I / GEORGE II / GEORGE III
REGENCY	1820–1830	GEORGE IV

(The term 'Regency' is actually used to cover the period 1800–1830 because George IV ruled as Prince Regent during the last ten years of his father's reign and also because the period saw great changes in design, especially of furniture.)

| WILLIAM IV | 1830–1837 | WILLIAM IV |
| VICTORIAN | 1837–1901 | VICTORIA |

Index

Adam, Robert, 34–5
Advertisements, 130
Aethelred (979–1016) King of England, 97
Aketon, 2
All Change, 102
Animal figures (Staffordshire pottery), 64–5
Antique Collectors' Club, 130–1
Antique fairs, 127–8
Antique shops, 124–6
Antiques: age definition, ix
  buying and collecting, 124–34
  buying and selling, 133–4
  fashions in, 131
  guarantees, 126
  investment value, x
  magazines on, xi
  scope, ix
Apostle Spoons, 77
Arks, 122
Armour, 1–6
  plate, 2–3
  sculptured monuments, 6
Armour-piercing weapons, 1
Arquebus, 11

Assay marks, 74–5, 77–8, 82
Assay Offices, 74–5, 82
Astbury, John, 67
Auction sales, 101, 128–30
  bidding at, 129–30
Augustus the Strong, King of Poland, 52–3, 54

Baker, Samuel, 128
Bargaining, 125
Barter, 93
Basket-hilted sword, 18
Bateman, Hester, 78
Bennett, Arnold, 63
Bentley, Thomas, 70
Bidding at sales, 129–30
Bigaglia, Pierre, 114–15
Böttger, Johann, 52, 53–4, 56
Boulle, André Charles, 35
Bolsover, Thomas, 81–2
Boulton, Matthew, 82–3
Bowie, James, 8–9
Bowie knife, 8–9
Bracelets, 106, 107
Bracket clocks, 87
Breast plate, 3
Britain, William, 120
Britannia, 99

[139]

British coins, 96–100
British Plate, 84
Brooches, 106
'Brown Besses', 13
Byrnie, 3

Cabinet-Maker and Upholsterers' Drawing Book (Sheraton), 33
Cabinet-Maker and Upholsterers' Guide, The (Hepplewhite), 32
Cabriole leg, 29
Cairngorm brooches, 111
Cameos, 111
Cane seated chairs, 30
Castellani of Rome (jeweller), 108
Cavalry swords, 19
Ceramics, xi
　marks, 132–3
Chelsea porcelain factory, 79
'China', 52
China, Bone, 57
　Feldspar, 58
　Stone, 58
Chinese porcelain, 47–51
　colourings, 48
　dynasties, 47–8
　export vessels, 50–1
　marks, 59
　symbolism, 48–9
Chinoiserie, 23
Chippendale, Thomas, 21–3

Chippendale furniture, 21–5
Christie, James, 128
Christie's, 128–9
Claymore, 18
Clichy paperweights, 115
Clocks, 87–92
　French, 90–2
Cnut, King of England, 98
Code Duello, 13–14
Coins, 93–103
　as a means of spreading information, 94–5
　auction sales, 101
　care of, 101
　collecting and buying, 100–1
　descriptions of condition, 101–2
　storing, 102–3
Coins and Medals, 102
Collections, 131
Collectors Guide, The, 127
Colt, Samuel, 14
Copeland, William Taylor, 58
Cornish soap-stone, 59, 61
Cotton, William (child labourer), 62
Crazing, 67
Cream ware (Queen's Ware), 69
Criminal figures (Staffordshire pottery), 66
Cross-bow, 1
'Crown of the rose' coin, 110–98–9
Cuirass, 1

[140]

Index

Daggers, 7-9
  ornamentation, 7
Dancing Hours vase, 71
Danegeld, 97
De Lamerie, Paul, 79
Diamonds, 104
Director (Chippendale), 22-3
Dirk, 7
Djeva, Z., 115
Dolls, 119-20
Dolls' house furniture, 118-19
Dolls' houses, 23, 118
Door knockers, 41-4
Door porters, 43-4
Dragoons, 12
Duelling pistols, 13-14

Ear-rings, 106, 107
Edgar (959-75) King of England, 97
Egyptian Black Basalt, 70
Electro Plating, 84-5
Elers brothers, 64
Elkington, 84
Emerson, James, 38
English Goldsmiths and Their Marks (Jackson), 79
Epergnes, 84
Etruria, 70
Etruscan work, 108
Exchange and barter, 93

Fairbottom, George, 81-2
Fairs, 127-8

Fakes, 132
  artificial crazing, 67
  furniture, 36, 132
  silver, 76
Farouk, King of Egypt, 116
Fitzwilliam Museum, Cambridge, x-xi
Flaxman, John, 71
Flint-lock pistols, 10-15
Florin, 98
Forgeries, 132
Furniture, 21-36
  authenticity of, 36
  fakes, 36, 132
  French, x, 35-6
  ornamentation of, 28-30, 33

Gadrooning, 83
Galeries du Louvre, 90
Garrick, David, 24
Gentleman and Cabinet-Maker's Director (Chippendale), 22-3
Gesso, 30
Giulliano of London (jeweller) 108
Gladius, 16-17
Glass, ix
  Venetian, 114
Goldsmiths' Company, 82-3
Gothic revival, 23-4
Graham, George, 88
Grandfather clocks, 88-9
Greek armour, 1
Greek coins, 93-4
Griffiths, John, 71

[141]

Gunners' stiletto, 7
Gunpowder, 11
Guns, 10–15

Half-crown, 99
Hallmarks, 74–6, 77–8
Hancock, Robert, 60
Hanley Museum, Stoke-on-Trent, xi
Harewood House, xi, 22, 24, 34
Harquebus see Arquebus
Harrison, John, 68
Hauberk, 3
Helmets, 3
Hepplewhite, George, 32
Hepplewhite furniture, 32–3
Hermitage Museum, Leningrad, 69
Horse brasses, 37–40

Import Duty, United States, ix
Inlaid furniture, 33

Jackson, Sir Charles, 79
Jambaias, 8
Japanning, 29–30
Jasper Ware, 70–2
Jet, 105–6
Jewellery, 104–12
  influence of archaeology, 107–8
Junk shops, 126–7

Kändler, J. J., 54
Kard, 8

Katars, 7
Kentucky Rifle, 14
Kenwood, 34
Key, Joseph, 46
Keys, 45–6
Khanjar, 8
Knee guards, 3
Knights: battle dress, 2–3
Kris, 19
Kukri, 19

Lacquering, 29–30
Lantern clocks, 87
Lascelles family, 21, 22
Lockets, 106
Locks, 45–6
Long-case clocks, 88–9
Louis XIV, 35
Louis XIV clocks, 90
Lutyens, Sir Edwin, 118

Mahogany clocks, 89
Mahogany furniture, 24
Mail coat, 1
Mail shirt, 3
Manchu porcelain, 47–8
Manufacture de Meubles de la Couronne, 35
Marco Polo, 47
Marquetry, 29, 89
Marwick, James, 88
Medicine figure, Chinese, 125–6
Meissen porcelain, 54–6
  marks, 54–6
Millefiori, 113
Ming porcelain, 47, 48, 52

Index

Mohurs, 99
Montgomerie, Archibald, 3-6
Museums, x
Musical clocks, 87-8

Necklaces, 106
Noah's arks, 122

Oak furniture, 26
Old Merchant's House, Great Yarmouth, 44
Opals, 109-11

Paperweights, 113-17
  modern, 116
Parian ware, 58
Paris Guild of Clockmakers, 90
Parure, 107
Peligot, Eugene, 115
Pendants, 106
Pew groups (Staffordshire pottery), 64
Pistols, 10-15
Poleyns, 3
Porcelain *see* Chinese, Meissen, Spode, Worcester import duty into Britain, 57
  marks, *see under type*
Portland, Duchess of, 72
Portland Vase, 71-3
Portobello Road street market, 130
Portrait coins, 95
Portrait jewellery, 105

Potteries, The, 63
Pottery: crazing, 67
Pratt, Felix, 65
Prattware, 65
Puritan Spoons, 77
Puritanism, 26

Queen's Ware, 69

Rapier, 18
Restorations, x
Revolvers, 14
Rings, 106
Rolled gold, 111
Roman coins, 94
Rupees, 100

Sabatons, 3
Sabellico, Marco Antonio, 114
Salt-glaze pottery, 64
Samurai swords, 20
Sanctuary, 41-2
Scott, Sir Walter, 7
Seal-Top Spoons, 77
Semi-precious stones, 109-11
Sheffield Plate, 81-6
  buying, 85-7
  cleaning, 85
Sheraton, Thomas, 33-4
Sheraton furniture, 33
Sherratt, Oliver and Martha 66-7
Short sword, 19
Silver, 74-80
  Britannia Standard, 76
  content, 76

[143]

Silver – *cont.*
  fakes, 76
  Irish, 79
  marks, 74–6, 77–78, 132
  period styles, 78
  Scottish, 79
  Sterling, 74
Silver Plate *see* Sheffield Plate
Smith, J., of Stockton, 72
Sotheby's, 128
Sovereign gold, 98
Sovereign's Champion, 4
Spatha, 17
Spode family, 57–8
Spode porcelain, 57–8
  marks, 58
Spoons, 77
Sprimont, Nicholas, 77
Staffordshire pottery, xi, 62–7
Stiletto, Gunners', 7
Street markets, 130
Sung porcelain, 48
Swein, King of Denmark, 97
Swords, 16–20
  dress, 18
Syon House, 34

Tiaras, 106
Toby jugs, 66
Tompion, Thomas, 88
Tournament, medieval: Victorian attempt at reconstruction, 4–6
Toy soldiers, 120–2
Toys, 118–23

Transfer printing (porcelain), 60
Tulwars, 19

Upholstery, 29

Veneering, 28, 29, 88–9
Venetian coins, 95
Venetian glass, 114
Victoria and Albert Museum, x, 23, 24, 25, 44, 77, 117
Viking coins, 97

Wall, Dr, 59
Wallace Collection, x
Walnut clocks, 88–9
Walnut furniture, 28–31
  periods and styles, 30
Walpole, Horace, 72
Walton, John, 66, 67
Watt, James, 82
Way, H. W. L., 115
Wedgwood, Josiah, 68–72
Wedgwood, Ralph, 72
Wedgwood pottery, xi, 68–73
  marks, 72
Wheel-lock pistol, 11–12
Whieldon, Thomas, 119
William the Conqueror, 98
Woburn Abbey, xi
Wood, Ralph and Aaron, 65, 67
Wooden animals, 122
Worcester porcelain, 59–61
  marks, 59–60, 61

Ysart, 116